4-17-62

61-15678

North Carolina in 1861

North Carolina in 1861

North Carolina in 1861

BY

JAMES H. BOYKIN

BOOKMAN ASSOCIATES | NEW YORK

MANUFACTURED IN THE UNITED STATES OF AMERICA BY
UNITED PRINTING SERVICES, INC.
NEW HAVEN, CONN.

MARIAE
GENITOR ET GENETRIX
FRATRES ET SORORES
DIVIUS

Contents

Introduction

MANY persons would contend that not only might truth arrived at scientifically not be final, but that the scientific method cannot even be applied to social phenomena. They assume that the data of human society are so fundamentally different from the data of the physical world and lower organic life that this method cannot be applied to the study of human relations. This is presumed to be true because of the contention that social data are too complex. A second reason why this method cannot be applied to a study of human society is the strong contention that social phenomena are subject to incalculable whims because of the presence in human beings of brains, will, mind, and soul. A third reason for rejecting the scientific method as a tool of research is expressed as the fear that, since the scientific method tends to be quantitative in its description, such description of human relations would omit various alleged qualitative conditions of an intangible nature which must be considered.

The scientific method has, nevertheless, proved itself incomparably superior to all other methods which man has employed in his age-old struggle to adjust himself to his environment. This method which has demonstrated its effectiveness in one field of human adjustment, the natural and biological sciences, should and can be employed even in those fields in which man's adjustment and control is relatively imperfect. Until the past thirty years, however, man made no serious attempt to apply the scientific method to social problems. The objections raised against this venture are not entirely valid. Not only must we distinguish between great difficulty and impossibility, but recognize that the "incalculable whims" that are present in social phenomena are present in natural phenomena as well. Scientific law meets this situtation by standardizing the conditions or abstracting the situation so that behavior may be described. The social scientists must find ways to accomplish this same goal.

"It would be unsound fancy and self-contradictory," Francis Bacon insisted, "to expect that things which have never yet been done can be done except by means which have never been tried." He pleaded that a method of intellectual operation be introduced "altogether better and more certain."

Every extension in the field of science has faced these same objections; and besides, even strictly historical method tends to merge gradually and to some extent objectively, into the methods of natural science. We must not forget, however, that because of the inherent limitation and influence of bias and prejudice on the sense perceptions, the work of the social scientist is more difficult. The main problem in the field of social science is, as Bacon suggests, that men "on their side must force themselves for a while to lay their notions by and begin to familiarize themselves with facts." He was convinced that "not much can be known in nature by the way which is now in use." It is "the peculiar and perpetual error of the human intellect to be more moved and excited by affirmatives than by negatives," he explained, but the intellect "ought properly to hold itself indifferently disposed toward both alike." In spite of his efforts, however, it is still true that, as Bacon concluded: "What a man had rather were true he more readily believes. . . ."

René Descartes joined Bacon in his noble effort when he said "the ground of our opinions is far more custom and example than any certain knowledge" and that which is probable, is "well nigh false." In his struggle to overcome his own preconceptions and prejudices, he said:

> I have never contemplated anything higher than the reformation of my own opinions, and basing them on a foundation wholly my own . . .

> But like one walking alone and in the dark, I resolved to proceed so slowly and with such circumspection, that if I did not advance far, I would at least guard against falling.

Because of their devotion to science, Bacon and Réne Descartes, in point of time, bridged the Renaissance to the modern era.

The writer has examined hundreds of newspapers, magazines, legislative journals, legislative and executive papers and documents, public laws and resolutions, convention ordinances, congressional records, court reports, deeds, wills, supreme court decisions, church minutes, convention minutes, conference journals, personal letters, personal collections, reports, memorials, and telegrams. The results of this research have been organized as brief reflections on some aspects of life in North Carlina between the early months of 1860 and the end of 1861. He has tried to be clear without using words that would persuade the reader, and to avoid colorful adjectives, vague and suggestive phrases, and words with strong emotional tones. In striving to establish the truth honestly and fairly on sound evidence, adverse evidence has been given the same weight as conforming evidence, even at the risk of having to change the hypothesis. Every effort has been made to guard against permitting coincidence to be mistaken for cause-and-effect relationships, thus enabling the writer to avoid the influence of subjectivity and prejudice. The final hypothesis arrived at in any scientifically conducted study cannot, in the absolute sense, be regarded as final truth. It represents only the best answer available with the present data. If it fails to meet the test of time and new discoveries, a better theory may supplant it.

Because of the nature of this report, the writer could not be expected to suggest a final hypothesis, yet since it covers the secession period in our history, he can no more escape the responsibility of raising this issue than he could be expected to arrive at a final solution to it. Thus the thesis he offers is in no way to be regarded as final.

An account of conditions in North Carolina exactly a century earlier, viewed in the light of conditions in 1961, is relevant and opportune. Both years are involved in eras of transition and within the transition North Carolina plays a unique role, a role which is not quite southern but by no means northern. In 1861, North Carolina drifted reluctantly and enigmatically into secession against her better judgment and against the welfare of her predominately agricultural yeomanry. Her moderation did not save her from the devastation of war, but left her free to enter more readily and more gracefully into the post-slavery era which followed the Civil War. In 1961, North Carolina opposes the ending of legal racial segregation with the same reluctance and misgiving, but again moderation prevails. It appears that North Carolina will move into the post-segregation era with grace and a minimum of discomfort and dislocation. As an example of what might be called both liberal moderation and/or conservative moderation, North Carolina at the beginning and end of a century of time demonstrates both the virtues and faults of moderation in social evolution. A study of North Carolina in 1861 must be instructive.

J. H. B.

PART I

Social History

Chapter One

Government and Population

NORTH CAROLINA in 1861 was a tobacco-producing, turpentine-distilling and slaveholding state. One of the original thirteen colonies, it was still not completely formed, because it had only eighty-six counties.[1]

There were several reasons why new counties were still being added. There were numerous requests for changes of boundary lines,[2] because many counties experienced difficulty over their county seats. Local officials sometimes failed to comply with the law in locating a place for the seat. Sometimes the necessary funds for construction of the courthouse were never collected. The people were sometimes dissatisfied with the location selected by the commissioners appointed for that purpose. Courts were sometimes held in private homes for which the owners were paid. When county seats for new counties were selected, it was often necessary to survey new county lines for the old county, since the old county seat was no longer in the center. Thus, Transylvania, Mitchell, and Clay Counties were added in 1861.[3]

A bill to lay off and establish the County of Transylvania, already passed in the House of Commons, was sent to the Senate on January 30. Received on February 1 by the upper house, it was ratified on February 15. This act and a supplemental act also ratified on that date[4] provided for the formation of the county from Henderson and Jackson Counties. Bounded on the west by South Carolina, its name is derived from *trans,* meaning across, and *sylva,* meaning woods.

An act providing for the establishment of Mitchell County was transmitted to the Senate on February 15 after it was signed by the speaker of the House,[5] and ratified on the following day.[6] It was organized out of territory ceded from Burke, Caldwell, McDowell, Watauga, and Yancey Counties and named in honor of Dr. Elisha Mitchell, a professor in the University of North Carolina.

The House was first to pass a bill providing for establishment of Clay County, but the Senate passed it with an amendment on February 16 and sent it back to the House, requesting concurrence.[7] It was ratified on February 20, and as in the case of Transylvania and Mitchell, a supplementary act followed and was ratified on February 25.[8] Formed out of the territory of Cherokee County, it was named in honor of Henry Clay.

Theoretically, all counties are equal, but the regulations governing the North Carolina counties then, as now, varied from place to place. Mitchell was to have no criminal jurisdiction, all such offenses to be under the jurisdiction of Burke, Caldwell, McDowell, Yancey, and Yatauga, the counties out of which it was formed. House Bill 42, introduced on August 21, sought to change its boundaries.[9]

A court of pleas and quarter sessions to be held by the justices of the peace of the county was established for Clay. The first term was to begin on the last Monday in May, the second on the last Monday in August, and the third on the last Monday in November. In 1862 and thereafter, they were to be held on the last Mondays in February, May, August, and November. The first term of the court was to be held "at the Methodist church near Fort Hembree in the said county and thereafter in such place in said county as the court may direct," until a courthouse was constructed and the seat of justice located. A majority of the acting justices of the peace in the first session were to elect a clerk, sheriff, coroner, "register entry taker," surveyor, and constable. They were to enter into bond as required by law and continue in office until successors were chosen and qualified according to acts of the General Assembly. Criminal offenses committed in Clay County were to continue under jurisdiction of Cherokee County until the superior court was established in Clay.[10]

Burton K. Dickey, William Walker, Drury Weeks, Pleasant Henry, and C. T. Rogers of Cherokee County were appointed commissioners by the Assembly "to select and determine the permanent seat of justice for said county" which was to be near the center. Ezekial Brown, James Coleman, R. B. Chambers, Will M. Sanderson, George Bristol, and John H. Johnson were to purchase or receive by donation for Clay County not less than twenty-five acres of land. A town called Haynesville, where the courthouse and jail were to be located, was to be laid out on this land. The land in the town was to be laid off in lots and sold at public auction "upon a credit of one, two, or three years." The sheriff was directed to collect what became due on these judgments. The temporary courthouse was to be replaced by a stone structure, to be paid for from the proceeds of the sale of lots, but the court was to tax the people to make up any deficiency in funds.[11]

Petitions were constantly being made to change or modify county lines but they were sometimes opposed. Eleven such petitions similar to the following one with forty-six signatures have been found.

Memorial

To the Hon the General assembly (sic) of North Carolina now in Cession. We the under Signed Citizens of Catawba County having understood that an application will be made to establish a new county taking a large portion of our said County of Catawba by running within 3./2 or 4 miles of the town of Newton which would be ruinous in its effects, and pray your Honorable body not to grant such a

county by taking any portion of our County as in duty
will ever pray (sic).[12]

Alleghany County citizens were not concerned about the
formation of counties, but too much legislation. Over one
of the longest arrays of signatures collected, they pleaded:

> . . . Your humble petitioners, Citizens of Said County, pray
> your Honorable Body not to have any more Legislation
> upon Said County as we your humble petitioners are fully
> satisfied with what has already been done, and we your
> petitioners will ever pray &c.[13]

The county sheriff was not only the chief law enforce-
ment official in the county, but was an important, if not
the most important tax official as well. The procedure was
for the sheriff to secure the tax lists from the county clerk
and by "attending the market place or other public square"
at various places in the county, to collect the taxes due.

Sheriff M. Master of Forsythe County announced on April
19 that he had received from the clerk of the county court
the list of taxables for the year ending December 31, 1860,
and was holding them ready for inspection. Meanwhile, he
requested all persons to inform him of any taxables which
might not be listed.[14]

Sheriff Hector McNeill of Cumberland County announced
on June 24:

> I will attend at the Market House in the Town of Fayette-
> ville, on Monday, the 1st Day of July next, for the purpose
> of collecting the Taxes due, on subjects taxed without
> being listed, viz:
>
> Circus riders, Stage players, Itinerant Singers, Insurance
> Companies, Billiard Tables, Bowling Allies, Livery Stables,
> Dentists, Portrait Painters, Venders of Playing Cards, Light-
> ning Rods, Auctioneers, Merchants, Ready Made Clothing,
> Patent Medicines, Peddlers, and Liquor Dealers. . . .

For those engaged or interested in "either branch of the above business," he appended the penalty section of the State Revenue Law. In announcing his schedule of visits in other parts of the county, the sheriff, who sometimes also announced visits to the county court house for this purpose, explained that persons who entered business were required to secure licenses before doing so.[15]

Tax collecting for the past year and tax listing for the coming year went on simultaneously. J. H. Roberts of Cumberland County announced on July 8 that he would be at the store formerly occupied by J. H. Roberts and Company "the balance of July" to take the tax lists and that no lists would be taken after that time.[16] Tax collecting did not seem to be proceeding satisfactorily in Fayetteville, because Deputy Sheriff R. W. Hardie announced on September 9 that he would "call personally upon the citizen tax payers of the town . . . during the present and ensuing week, to collect the same."[17]

Sheriff J. R. Grady of Harnett County announced on July 8 that he would meet the citizens of the county in the various districts for the purpose of collecting 1860 taxes. Not only did he notify the taxpayers "to attend and settle their taxes, unless they wish their propery sold," but he also announced that the candidates for clerk of the county and superior courts would be present to address them. He listed his politicking tax-collecting schedule as follows:

> Barbecue, Monday, July 22
> Upper Little River, Tuesday, July 23
> Stewart's Creek, Wednesday, July 24
> Grove, Thursday, July 25
> Mill's Creek, Friday, July 26
> Buckhorn, Saturday, July 27.[18]

State concern over revenue was expressed at the end of 1860 when Willie J. Palmer, Secretary of the Board of

Trustees of the North Carolina Institution for the Deaf and Dumb and the Blind, sent the names of the students and the cost of maintaining them to the sheriffs of the following counties: Chatham, October 21; Cumberland, December 3; and Catawba, December 25, 1860; Bladen and Cumberland, January 1; Cabarrus, January 3; Cumberland, January 8; and Davie, April 28, 1861. These sheriffs were to send one copy of Palmer's notice to the chairman of the county court and return one to Palmer to be deposited with the secretary of state. The county justices were required to levy a tax equal to the cost of maintaining and training the students from their county for the year ending on the following June 30. This procedure was to be repeated in successive years and the funds collected were to be paid to the Institution.[19] Palmer, who was principal of the school, sent a message, dated February 1, 1861, to the Honorable H. T. Clark, Speaker of the Senate, inviting the officers and members of the Senate to be present at an exhibition of the deaf, mute, and blind pupils of the institution that night in the chapel of the school.[20] In addition to indicating the progress of the pupils and the school, the exhibitions had other obvious purposes: to show how the state funds were being spent and to encourage tax payment.

The Assembly ratified a bill on February 23, 1861, amending the 1859 revenue law. It exempted state property, property set aside for agricultural fairs, and property used for churches and religious societies, but taxed various business interests. It sought to tax slaves but failed.[21] A tax of one-half of one per cent was finally imposed on both resident and non-resident slave traders in North Carolina on September 23, 1861.[22]

By mid-June, 1861, there was a general feeling in the New Bern section that the Convention should hasten, complete its work, and adjourn. "The war debt of the State will be heavy even should it end in a few months," the *Newbern*

Progress wrote, "and the resources of our people and of the State will be strained to the utmost, and hence the need for economy in every branch of the public service. . . ."[23]

". . . It would seem that our expenditures for the war have already been very heavy," the state treasurer reported to the Assembly on August 17, "but . . . all drafts for the support of it have been promptly met at this office." He recommended that the revenue law be amended to increase the revenue for the following year, beginning July 1, 1862, at least 25 per cent.[24] This increase in revenue was necessary, if we are to take the advice of one who should know, because C. H. Brogden, State Comptroller, wrote the speaker and members of the House on August 28 regarding this issue. He pointed out that never before had North Carolina had three sessions of the legislature and two conventions in one year. Then he said that under the strain of mounting duties and responsibilities, he was requesting more help for his office from the legislature.[25]

In the regular session of the 1860-61 Assembly, a struggle developed over efforts to divide the state into eight districts. The House voted 55 to 26 to divide the state into eight districts on Februray 4.[26] One such bill passed the second reading in the Senate on February 15 and was read the second time on February 22 but again was lost.[27]

House Bill 67 and Senate Bill 63, designed to divide the state into ten congressional districts, were introduced in both houses between August 24 and September 2. The Senate reported that it had passed the bill in a message dated August 30 and signed by L. W. Humphrey, Speaker Pro Tempore of the Senate, but it could not be ascertained precisely which bill it was. House Bill 67 also specified how the senators and congressmen of the Confederate States of America were to be chosen. The bill gave special attention to selection of the senators, but it specified that the Assembly should "elect such senator *viva voce* by a majority of the

joint votes of both houses." The senator-elect was to receive
a certificate of election signed by the speakers of the two
houses and be commissioned by the governor under the seal
of the State.[28] An act based on one such bill was ratified on
September 4.[29]

Because of strong support in favor of this act, in favor
of dividing the state into districts, or because of political
expediency, action was taken two weeks later to further
divide the state. A bill to divide the state into twelve election
districts was read three times, ordered enrolled in the Senate
on September 18,[30] and was ratified two days later.[31]

Even after the state was divided into twelve districts, there
seems to have been some divergence of opinion as to whether
North Carolina should elect one or two senators. W. T.
Dortch sent a message to the speaker of the Senate dated
August 27 and proposing to go into election of two Con-
federate States senators, but on the following day he wrote
the speaker of the Senate that the House did not concur in
the Senate proposal to elect two senators at twelve noon,
but proposed to elect one senator at twelve noon. In the
August 28 House message, the Senate was informed that
"Person, Outlaw, Bragg, Graham, Clingman, Avery, D. S.
Reid, E. G. Reade, Morehead, and Osborne" were in nomination. The Senate concurred in the plan to vote for one
Confederate senator, and added to the list of nominees the
name of George Davis.

The vote for senator was taken on August 29 and again on
September 6, when the Senate refused to consider the election. Concurrence to elect was achieved on September 10
at 11:00 A.M., but again no candidate received a majority.
The vote was taken again that afternoon, with the same
results. There was no majority on September 11 nor September 12. Dortch sent a second message to the Senate on September 12, proposing to consider election of two Confederate
senators, and a second election that afternoon and three

elections on the following day yielded Davis sixty-five votes in the House. Meanwhile on the latter day, the Senate reported that Dortch had received seventy-one votes and was duly elected. Fifty-five of the votes for Dortch were received in the House.[32] George Davis of New Hanover County and William T. Dortch of Wayne County, duly elected in the Second Extra Session of the North Carolina Assembly, thus qualified along with the state's ten representatives in the First Congress, First Session, of the Confederate States of America.

Whether because of conservatism, stubbornness, or backwardness, the Assembly either never thought of making certain changes or steadfastly refused to do so. It refused to adjourn to Wilmington, even in the face of one of the worst smallpox epidemics. Never, until 1861, did it provide any flag for the State capitol. By 1861, it was discovered that the Assembly would need better heating facilities for the capitol, but Senate Resolution 98 which would have authorized Governor John W. Ellis to have coal grates placed in the fireplaces of the Senate Chamber, in the Hall of the House of Commons, and in the rooms of the public offices, was tabled on January 21. An act providing for heating and lighting the capitol, ratified on January 26, 1861, directed the State treasurer to employ "some suitable persons to have the halls and such other rooms of the capitol as they think expedient comfortably heated by a furnace or some other suitable manner, and lighted with gas." The cost was to be paid out of money "in his hands not otherwise appropriated." The estimated cost was approximately $2,500, but on May 9 the Assembly repealed the Act.[33]

In the 1860-61 session of the Assembly, a committee on adjournment at Christmas was appointed. In December, it presented a resolution providing that a general leave of absence be granted to all such members as chose to accept it from and after Thursday, December 20, 1860, until Monday, January 7, 1861. The Committee recommendations also provided that no bill or resolution of a public nature be acted upon from December 20 to January 7. The House changed the latter date to January 2, and passed the Resolution 62 to 55 on December 18.[34] A motion was introduced on December 20 that adjournment be extended to January 7 and it was passed by a vote of 63 to 29.[35] A Senate resolution was presented on December 18 and 19, but it failed.[36] The House met from December 21 to January 7, but since no quorum was present, adjourned each day. The Senate met Friday, December 21, but from Saturday, December 22 to Tuesday, January 1 adjourned, no quorum being present.[37]

In a night session on Monday, January 28, a resolution to send a message to the Senate early Tuesday morning, proposing to adjourn the Assembly to Wilmington or some other point to finish the business then before it due to the spread of smallpox in Raleigh, was presented in the House. It was lost by a vote of 41 to 36. A resolution that a committee be appointed to see that those members and assistant doorkeepers who visited those ill with smallpox be vaccinated at once was presented, but it failed to pass.[38] A resolution that any House member exposed to smallpox, either by being with any person ill with that disease, or near enough to incur the risk of catching the contagion have leave of absence and be requested to absent himself until danger was passed, was introduced in the House. The House moved to strike out Wilmington and insert Newbern [sic] but the bill failed to pass. A motion was made to strike out Wilmington and insert Fort Macon, but that motion was also lost.

A resolution to provide a United States flag for the capitol was lost, 62 for and 49 against it in the House (a two-thirds vote required) on December 18.[39] House Bill 239, introduced by Samuel P. Hill of Caswell County on June 10, 1861, provided for the purchase of a State flag. It was lost,

59 for and 48 against it.[40] Josiah Turner of Orange County moved that the Senate take up a resolution which he had offered and which had been tabled concerning the raising of a United States flag on the State capitol on January 31. His motion was lost 32 to 16.[41]

While the North Carolina Assembly was struggling to prevent having a flag on the capitol, a Raleigh newspaper reported on April 24 that the flag of the Confederate States of America had been run up on the capitol of North Carolina.[42]

To fully understand why the Assembly failed to enact any flag legislation, it must be remembered that the Assembly was the regular legislative body, that the Convention was an emergency body expected to take emergency action, and that it was pro-secessionist. These convention delegates were pro-Confederate, because it was not necessary to call a convention to remain in the Union and it was understood that to favor a convention was to favor secession. Thus, it was expected that the "fire-eaters," or extreme pro-Confederates, would make the best delegates to the convention, and they were predominant.

Perhaps it was the fire-eaters who were bold enough to run up the Confederate flag on the capitol before North Carolina seceded, but it is certain that it was the Convention which voted to design a State flag, This flag, as provided for by the first session of the State convention, consisted of a red field with a white star in the center, and an inscription above the star. This was included in a semi-circle at the top, formed by the words "May 20, 1775," date of the Mecklenburg Declaration of Independence, and a semi-circle below the star formed by the words "May 20, 1861."[43] The only difference between the North Carolina flag then and now seems to be that the field is now blue, not red, the first bar is red, not blue, and April 12, 1776, has replaced the North Carolina date of secession in the lower semi-circle.

The Assembly in 1861, as now, had to face a flood of petitions concerning almost every conceivable problem. North Carolina was greatly in need of roads, particularly in the west. In November, 1860, a petition from the citizens of Jackson County referred to "the want of a good waggon [sic] way or Turpentine Road through the southern end of the county." The "said line" suggested, the petitioners explained, would be most practical "for giving the sd [sic] village of Fairfield and Hog Back a connection with the roads in the Valley of French Broad River."[44] A Jackson County road leading through Fairfield and Hog Back Vallies was only one of several proposals, because the Assembly took action to improve or locate three roads in February, 1861. The Assembly passed an act to lay off, locate, and establish a road from Statesville in Iredell County to Wilkes County on February 22.[45] An act to improve the road from John Allen's to the top of Blue Ridge Mountain at or near Fisher's Gap in Surry County was ratified on February 23, when the Assembly appropriated five thousand dollars for that purpose.[46] On February 25, legislative provision was made for improving the public road from Taylorsville to Boon by way of Russel's Gap and Holdman's Ford. Three thousand dollars was appropriated for that project.[47]

A petition, originated at Shelby on December 31, 1860, indicated that the petitioners had about four years previously buried each of their children on the land of William Vaughn, temporarily but with his consent. They intended and expressed their determination to move them as soon as a family burial ground could be secured. They showed that since that time the said Vaughn, brother-in-law of the petitioners, "through contrary and wicked motives," refused to let them remove the bodies or remains of their dead children, "contrary to right and every law of humanity. Therefore, they pray your honorable body to pass a law granting them the privilege to go to said burial ground and remove the ashes of their once dear children, and as in duty bound they will ever pray."

The petition was signed by Eusebius Hendrick and Chapel Hendrick and terminated with the following endorsement and forty-four signatures:

> We, the undersigned, know the petitioners and know that they are men of good character and believe that they should be permitted to remove the remains of their children as prayed for in justice to their children and their own wishes, and recommend the passage of the act prayed for.[48]

On January 15, 1861, Senate Bill 90, "A Bill to Pemit Persons to Remove the Remains of their deceased Relatives When Buried Upon the Land of Another," was introduced in the Senate. It was read and passed on that date, but on January 17, the Committee on Propositions and Grievances recommended that it not pass. On February 1 it was again read and passed and on February 23 it was read and tabled. No legislation on cemeteries was enacted in the regular, first or second sessions of the Assembly, nor the first or second Convention.

In addition to the regular Assembly which opened on November 19, 1860 and adjourned on February 25, 1861, the first extra session of the Assembly and the Convention were in session during May and June, 1861, and the second extra session of the Assembly and the Convention were in session during August and September. The second extra session of the Assembly opened on August 15. By 6:00 on the evening of September 23, in response to a Senate message, N. N. Fleming, Secretary of the House of Commons, wrote the secretary of the Senate that the House had also completed its business and would, in pursuance of a joint resolution adjourn *sine die* on return of the messenger.[49]

Petitions for pardon, employment, or commissions, home defense legislation, and assistance from other States were sent directly to the governor. Far more petitions were sent to the governor than to the Assembly because, unlike the legislators, he was continuously in Raleigh throughout his two-year tenure and long before the Civil War had become a symbol of justice to the oppressed.

John W. Ellis of Rowan County served his first term as governor from January 1, 1859 to January 1, 1861 and succeeded himself for a second term. He died in office on July 7, and Henry T. Clark of Edgecombe County, Speaker of the Senate, succeeded him. Apparently there was no regular inauguration date. On December 20, 1860, the Senate ordered Clark to send a message to the House proposing "a joint select committee" of two from the Senate and three from the House to "wait on his excellency, the Governor" and ascertain when it would suit his convenience to appear before the House of Commons of the General Assembly and take the oath of office. Such a committee would have also been ordered to make suitable arrangements for the reception of his Excellency "at such time as he may designate to take the oath of office."[50] This was ten days before his tenure expired.

On May 1, 1861, a letter from Greensboro and one from Salem were addressed to Ellis, requesting that he pardon Moses Smith, Jr., who had been convicted of murdering James M. Vass in Forsythe County Superior Court. The Greensboro letter described Smith as "greatly afflicted, feeble, badly humpbacked, much deformed and crooked." The letter informed the governor:

> I understand the community desire (*sic*) his pardon but as to that you will be informed by the petition from the county.
> On account of his deformity and feeble state of health, I have much sympathy for him and shall certainly say nothing against the movement of his friends for a pardon.

The Salem petition said in part that ". . . My apology for deviating from a consistent course of not interfering with the regular course of law" is "for the sake of aged parents, bowed down by the harrowing thought that their son, from childhood a cripple, would die a felon's death."[51] A letter from Will Floyd of Old Town, dated May 4, urged clemency for Smith on the grounds that he was respectable, had a large family, and was "one of the most deformed, most hump- or crooked-back beings I ever saw." C. L. Banner, in a petition from Salem, also on May 4, asked clemency for Smith. Banner described Smith as a "poor, miserable man who, when he was young, had his back injured by a fall which prevented further growth of his body." His arms and legs grew to their proper proportion, however, "thus making him a very deformed creature."[52] There were seven other petitions on behalf of Smith who was to be executed on May 17, but no document could be found indicating that he had been pardoned.

Robert Reinhardt was convicted of manslaughter in the spring, 1861, term of the Lincoln County Superior Court and sentenced to six months in prison. Four grounds for pardon were listed in a petition from Catawba County citizens, urging executive clemency: the extreme youth of the prisoner, who was only eighteen when he committed the offense; his good character, both before and after he committed the offense; the age, worth, and high respectability of his parents; and "his voluntary return to abide by the laws of his country." Governor Ellis granted pardon on May 3.[53]

A petition, signed on May 3 from Northampton County, requested the governor to extend executive clemency to "negro boy Jeff the property of James V. Sauls, tried and convicted of the murder of negro slave Sam [sic] . . ." at the spring term of Superior Court. The petitioners were satisfied that the defendant did not intend to kill when he struck the victim and that he had "an excellent character for obedience, humility, and strict devotion to the work of his master in behalf of whose property the difficulty arose which places him in the position he now stands."

Signed at Jackson, the petition bore the signatures of forty-five persons, including eight jurors, William T. Buxton, Clerk of Superior Court, Dr. C. G. C. Moon, Dr. W. S. Copeland, and the county sheriff. This pardon was also granted on May 3.[54]

J. C. Fry, convicted of horse stealing and sentenced to "thirty-nine lashes on his bare back," to be kept in jail for three months, and to receive "thirty-nine more lashes and turned out," was denied clemency on May 15.[55]

In her efforts to secure release from the armed services of a close relative, apparently her son, Mrs. Frances Timberlake on May 8 wrote the following letter to Governor Ellis:

> honorable Sir:
>   I seat myself to drop you a few lines to beg you to let Francis P. Timberlake off I am a widow and being in a house by myself and you will do me great favor if you will let him off I beg you with all the simethy that is in my Power I wish to do right if I know how I hope that you will have compassion on me I am getting old and I have bin left a widow and have rase my children and have see great deal of trouble I hope dear sir that you will have compassion on me and let him off
>
> Youse with respect
Frances Timberlake
>
> Please direct your letter to Roxboro[56]

On May 23, Governor Ellis received four telegrams, all from outside North Carolina, requesting aid. One was from John Letcher, Governor of Virginia, and the others were from General W. Gwynn. Gwynn's first message was a request for one hundred thousand caps, "or as many as you can spare." A longer message from Gwynn who was at Norfolk informed Ellis that he had been authorized from Richmond to call upon Ellis for "all the troops I may need." Gwynn said his requirement was at least four thousand men, but Gwynn added, "I am without amunition or caps equipages— Troops without these requirements would be in my way. . . . The Enemy still reinforcing and action."[57]

M. S. Perry, Governor of Florida, wrote Ellis on June 7 that he had commissioned the Honorable James Blanks, special agent of Florida, to request that North Carolina furnish Florida four hundred muskets.[58] On the following day, T. T. Long of Florida was introduced by V. R. Gist, Adjutant General of South Carolina, by letter to Governor Ellis in an effort to secure arms.[59]

Meanwhile Ellis was called upon to aid those struggling with the fine arts and other seeking commissions in the army or positions of various kinds. On the same eventful May 23, T. M. Jones of Greensboro Female College wrote the Governor:

> Permit me to introduce . . . Prof. W. C. A. French of Greensboro Female College. He is Professor of Oil Painting.
> He desires to visit South Carolina for the purpose of making arrangements for painting a national picture representing the raising of the Flag upon Fort Sumpter. . . .
> Any assistance that you may afford him . . . will be highly appreciated by him, and confer a favor upon me.[60]

Colonel H. N. Howard wrote from "Head Quarters [sic] 39th Regt NCM Smithville N. C. [sic]" to Adjutant General J. F. Hoke, that it was his "pleasant duty" to inform him that a company known as the "Brunswick Guard" had been organized in the county, and "are now at Smithville provided for at county expense." He said they were tendering their services to "the Govener [sic] to aid in defending the honor . . . of the state & are now awaiting terms and orders." Following was a list of the officers and men.[61]

Harry E. Cotton of Wilmington addressed a letter to "His Excellency, Hon. Jno. W. Ellis and Messrs. Winslow, Guion and Bradford" on May 18. He said he wished to serve in the

Regular Army of North Carolina and "would respectfully tender myself to you as a candidate for the Post of Captain." He said he would raise a company of able-bodied men, well-suited for riflemen in a short time after receiving the commission, "if you are disposed to tender it to me." In concluding his letter, Cotton wrote:

> I have sent no recommendations as a majority of the Board are acquainted with me and I am known throughout the State. I never drink any intoxicating liquors nor do I indulge in any dissipation.
>
> Very Respectfully
HARRY E. COTTON
>
> P.S. My military training has been a thorough one in one of our volunteer Rifle Companies.[62]

When W. W. Pierce wrote Governor Ellis from Raleigh on the eventful May 20, asking him to confirm his appointment to the rank of captain by General W. H. Whiting however, on the reverse side of the page was a letter of endorsement signed by five persons. The second letter was dated May 21.[63]

Not only was it apparent that the state required no specific qualifications for officers of the army, those seeking positions sometimes doubted their own qualifications. Ellis clarified this in his answer to a Salisbury letter on May 24. N. N. Fleming wrote on that date that he was desirous "of being of some service to the country in the present emergency." He said that if he could get a commission as captain in the state troops he would "try to raise a company." Although "I have no experience," he explained, "I hope to be able to render myself competent for the position, or at least as nearly so as many others whose services will have to be called . . . for the want of better." Due to "the great numbers who have already volunteered from this county," he said it would be difficult to recruit a company. If he could have the privilege of selecting the other officers "with a view to their competency as well as their efficiency in raising the company, I hope to be able to succeed. I believe that I can be of more service as an officer than as a private." Fleming requested an early reply, because court was to be held on the following week and he considered that a good time to canvass for men.[64] Fleming was promised the commission, because hurriedly written on the back of his letter were the following instructions:

Tell him he shall be appointed if he shall raise a company —That companies are constantly tendered and appointments are now made in that way.[65]

The officers of a company consisted of one captain, one first lieutenant, one second lieutenant, one third lieutenant, and sometimes one ensign.[66] The Rev. Samuel Pearce of Hillsboro, minister of the Methodist Episcopal Church, South, wrote Ellis on May 29, for a chaplaincy. He said he was prepared to administer the ordinances of religion to "the well, afflicted, sick or dying" [sic], and in a separate paragraph he added:

I heartily Endorse [sic] the present War of the South for Southern Rights and Independence.

Endorsements were added to the letter and Pearce wrote again on the same sheet on June 18, transmitting the endorsements to the governor.[67]

Miss N. H. Whitfield of Enfield wrote on July 1, requesting an appointment as nurse for soldiers, and asked that the governor authorize "sisters of mercy" for that purpose.[68]

Meanwhile, Eugene M. Williams, "Captain of the Jeff. Davis Cadets" referred to the organization of "another military company risen up in Newberne [sic]" composed of young men and "consisting of forty-eight rank and file." He said they had organized and elected officers and were willing to purchase their own uniforms and necessary equipment, but Captain Williams added:

> I, therefore, write to you asking if you can furnish us with arms 'tis [sic] all we ask . . . if you can do so you will never have cause to regret.[69]

G. W. Blackwell of Kittrell Springs suggested to the governor that able-bodied men engaged in cooking and other similar duties be replaced "by persons exempt from military duties." He also suggested that free Negroes would gladly do the work for a small compensation and that insurrection would be lessened in proportion to the number of free blacks taken from each county.[70]

Thus many volunteers wished to serve their country, but as officers. They themselves sometimes doubted their qualifications, while the governor stated no specific ones, except that they should raise a company.

Among the patriots were William L. Robinson and W. J. Houston. Robinson wrote to J. R. Beaman, Clerk of the Sampson County Court, on May 10 from his Taylor's Bridge residence, resigning his office as one of the justices of the peace for Sampson County, because, he said, "justice is hard to obtain & Peace Seems to have fled the land." To obtain justice by the sword, he explained, and "to conquer a peace" was his motto.[71]

There were scores of other similar resignations, but the resignation of W. J. Houston was far less usual. Writing from Raleigh on May 29, he informed Governor Ellis that he was resigning his commission as a member of the Convention for several reasons. He said he doubted that he had the right to hold his commission without resigning his position as solicitor, and had applied for "a place of much less rank in active service." Being a member of the Convention, he said he was "daily admonished" that he was doing injustice "to your excellency [sic], to my constituents, and my health by attempting the discharge of both."[72] The absence from home of most of the able-bodied men led to problems of home defense. Governor Ellis was informed in a letter from J. H. Foust of Reed Creek in Randolph County on June 10, that he had information from reliable sources that a band of desperate men had organized into "a compact for the general purpose of plunder as soon as the volunteers leave for service."[73] J. J. Bricknell and J. P. Lovelace of Wilkes County reported on June 15, various illegal activities such as violence, plundering of meat houses, breaking into residences, and theft of money. The desperadoes defied the sheriff's deputies and would not submit to arrest, making it necessary for some persons to be killed in the process. Both Bricknell and Lovelace applied to Ellis for instructions as to what to do in such cases and asked whether they should be committed to the county jail or sent to the army. They requested that the governor commission a home guard "here at Lovelace" and that blank commissions be sent by return mail, if possible. They said they intended to form the company with old men, but family heads "of good moral character [sic] law abiding men [sic] whole soul southern rights men."[74] On June 22, J. P. Aldridge and others informed the governor that there were abolitionists in the county who defied and molested the home guard. Writing from Franklinville, Randolph County, Aldridge said his information was that they had no power to molest these abolitionists. They had made threats as to what they would do when the volunteers left, and Aldridge was requesting authority to "clear out such fiends as them."[75]

Between early January and mid-summer, 1861, North Carolina was increasingly involved in the war. A special train from Wilmington arrived in Raleigh on January 1, bearing a committee consisting of the Honorable W. S. Ashe, Captain E. D. Hall, and two other men who were referred to as Messieurs Larinet and Hedrick. This committee was to consult the governor "on the propriety of taking Fort Johnson on the Cape Fear River about two miles from its mouth."[76] A letter from W. R. Burbank, Corresponding Secretary of the Safety Committee, addressed Ellis from Washington on May 10. The letter stated that there were three vessels ashore on our coast, one loaded with sugar near Cape Hatteras, one with molasses, and another near Currituck Inlet, with railroad iron. The purpose of Burbank's letter was to secure instructions as to whether "the people on the northeast section of our shore" should seize them in the name of the state.[77] A petition to the governor, dated May 20, stated that fifty Craven County citizens had taken possession of a vessel in North Carolina waters "owned by parties in New Yourk [sic]." The signers were petitioning Ellis "not to release said vessel," because, they explained, "if you would do so, no human eye can foresee the consequences." This correspondence contained a second petition attached which indicated the presence of one or more vessels owned in part by persons in New York "and other yankey [sic] towns," all being loaded with spirits of turpentine and other naval stores. It petitioned the governor to "forbid any shipment of the above articles being made from this port North."[78] These petitions seem to have had different purposes, the first to prevent the release of ships and the second to prevent current and subsequent shipment of certain products to the North. An embarrassing conflict of jurisdiction seems to have been expressed in a letter by Bartholomew of Raleigh to Thomas Ruffin. He said his department seemed to have had jurisdiction over all matters of equipment prior to May 20 and of such equipment since that date over which no other department had jurisdiction, and added: "I have never been so embarrassed."[79]

On July 7, 1861, for the first time in the history of the state, North Carolina deplored the death of a governor. The Honorable John W. Ellis died at the Red Sulphur Springs,

Virginia, on that date. The Honorable Henry T. Clark, Speaker of the Senate, assumed the administration of the affairs of state. W. T. Dortch wrote to the Speaker of the Senate on September 26 that the House had resolved that a message be sent to the Senate proposing appointment of a "joint select committee" of three from the Senate and five from the House to "inquire into the provision of the Constitution" of North Carolina relative to the vacancy of the office of governor and "report whether the duty devolves on the Assembly to fill the vacancy" occasioned by the death of Ellis. Senate Bill 107 directed the public treasurer to pay Clark the salary of the Governor from the date he assumed responsibility.[80]

When Clark addressed the Assembly on August 16, he said that although some counties had sent few men, some had sent more than their quota. He explained that it was the North Carolina policy to equip volunteers "with every comfort consistent with our means." North Carolina had been flattered with the compliment that it had sent the best equipped troops that had gone to Virginia, he said; then he listed the needs of the state. The Convention had postponed the issuing of the treasury notes authorized by the Assembly until March 1, 1862. Meanwhile, it had permitted the treasurer to borrow three million dollars from the banks, less the amount already loaned under the act passed by the Assembly in Extra Session. Much of that money had been spent, Clark said, and the additional sum to be borrowed, he feared, was more than the banks would be prepared to loan.

He said that the system of exemptions was very detrimental and urged that the Assembly require the same duty of all. He said this duty would then be "more cheerfully submitted to" and mentioned the militia as one of the main instruments of a free country.

Confessing dependence on the North, Clark said the blockade of the North Carolina coast established two important facts: North Carolina had become almost entirely dependent on the North in its commercial relations, but had the means and materials for supplying all of the needs he enumerated within its borders.[81]

On September 11, Governor Clark wrote the Assembly that the old government, the United States, was simply asking for men and providing clothing, equipment, and subsistence, but that the condition of the Confederacy was such that the State should equip and clothe its volunteers. Justice to the state required a rigid accounting of all expenditures of public funds, he said, and under the great pressure of buying then developing, it seemed necessary to establish an auditor's office to examine and pass on the resulting accounts. This problem he urged the Convention to consider seriously before it adjourned.[82]

Chapter Two

Advertisement, Business, and Trade

THERE was a tremendous amount of trade carried on in North Carolina in 1861, but the courts made no distinction between the sale and transfer of real estate and slaves, and little, if any, distinction between the transfer of real estate and various other types of property.

In a cause removed from the Court of Equity of Craven County in the fall of 1860, John R. Riggs, indebted to Seth Muse for the sum of $702.50, made an indenture to Muse for two Negro slaves, Abram and Joe, as security, and at the same time took from Muse a deed of defeasance. The defendant insisted on the statute requiring contracts concerning slaves to be in writing as a bar to the plaintiff's equity. After losing in Craven, Riggs appealed the judgment to the State Supreme Court. The Supreme Court ruled that an objection that the declaration of trust was not in writing and therefore void was not found tenable. It cited *Shelton* v. *Shelton,* 58 North Carolina, 292, a land case, and ruled that in that case the subject was land, in the 1860 case it was a slave, but that there was no distinction between land and slaves.[1]

Julius Miller who was operating a general store at 18 Fayetteville Street in Raleigh, sold to Moses Hecht on November 9, 1860, for $2,150, all of his dry goods, jewelry, ready-made clothing, boxes, hats, boots, shoes, store furniture, and utensils, "together with the lease running to 1st January next," and "also one negro woman named Sarah and her child."[2] The sale was made by deed now registered in the

Wake County Courthouse. S. M. Williams sold to G. W. Norwood on September 6, 1860, for $1,500 "Margaret, a woman about 22, and her two children—John, a boy about 4 years old and Salina, a girl about 2 months," by indenture.[3] Jackson Moss transferred ownership of one billiard table to John Boylan by deed on November 15, 1860.[4] Thomas W. Younge acknowledged payment of $80.00 for a sorrel mare from James J. Syms and C. P. Wilder, and $135.00 from Benjamin M. Carpenter for a horse sold on November 19, 1860, by indenture.[5]

Dionius Jackson conveyed to A. Y. Bailey land, three feather beds, three chairs, and other furniture, cattle, hogs, and one stack of fodder in a single indenture on March 22, 1861.[6] Dempsey Sorrell, in an indenture dated July 26, 1861, "for love and affection" bequeathed to Alvis Sorrell "a certain negro boy named Wilson about 23 . . . and one one hundred and one thirty-six acre tracts of land," the conveyance to take effect on his death.[7]

The major medium of advertising was the newspaper. Advertisements in the *Daily Bulletin* and the *Catawba Journal* published at Charlotte, the *Bulletin* announced, afforded unusual advantages to advertisers, "both home and abroad." They commanded "a circulation medium of over three thousand copies per week," the *Bulletin* explained, "which we have no doubt are read by at least ten thousand."[8]

Slaves who had run away from their masters were arrested, confined to jail, and exposed to public auction to pay the fees as directed by law,[9] but as full-scale war developed, employers depended on the newspapers to help them locate workers of various sorts. William Johnson, President of the Atlantic, Tennessee, and Ohio Railroad, advertised for six slaves to work on his railroad.[10] Robert H. Cowan, Secretary of the Wilmington, Charlotte, and Rutherford Railroad, announced on May 15 that the position of master mechanic for the railroad would be filled by the directors at their regular meeting in Charlotte on May 21. "The salary," the announcement said, "will not exceed $1200 per annum."[11] "Wanted to hire 50 Negro men to work on the Western Railroad," T. S. Lutterloh announced on October 21," and "10 four horse wagons to haul coal from Egypt Shaft to McIver's depot."[12] Lutterloh seemed to have faced some difficulty in securing the workers, because on December 30 he announced:

Wanted to Hire
50 NEGRO MEN to work at Grading
on Western Railroad.[13]

D. D. French of Lumberton on November 15 advertised for "a person who understands stilling both Corn and Rye Whiskey" whom he said would "receive immediate and constant employment."[14]

Northern merchants continued to advertise in the southern newspapers and periodicals. News from the North was obtained through exchanges. Livingston and Company of Pittsburgh, Pa., advertised farm grist mills and corn shellers. Daniel F. Beatty of Washington, New Jersey, advertised, "New Pianoes, $125, $135, and Upward. New Organs, $65 to $440."

S. J. Hinsdale and Company advertised "White Kerosene Oil Price $125 Gallon [sic]" as early as June, 1860.[15] During late 1860 and early 1861, one advertiser, trading as Mrs. Gibson, announced "To the Ladies" that "Mrs. Gibson respectfully informs her friends and the public generally . . . she is prepared to make DRESSES in the most fashionable style." She had taken the agency for the sale of the "new chart for cutting ladies' dresses" and one for boys' clothing. Ladies were requested to call and see them at her residence "on Hay Mount, the fifth residence above the Protestant Church" in Fayetteville.[16] E. Lilly, advertising fall and winter goods at Floral College, North Carolina, of-

fered his stock of jerseys, blankets, Negro brogans, ladies'
dress goods, silk and velvet bonnets, and ready-made clothing.[17] George Brandt was manufacturing clothing on Hay
Street in Fayetteville. His advertisement appeared regularly,
urging support of home industry.[18] The *Carolina Watchman*
published a notice to sheriffs, stating that tax receipts could
be neatly printed to order and put in books if desired "at
short notice and on moderate terms."[19] Lists of letters held
at the post office were published in the newspapers at peri-
odic intervals,[20] but far more sophisticated was the E. J. Hale
and Sons advertisement of standard literature. Included in
this list were *The Works of Charles Lamb,* five volumes,
edited by Talfourd; *The Works of Oliver Goldsmith,* four
volumes; *Fenelon's Works; Hood's Comic Miscellanies;* Cur-
rer Bell's works; *Jane Eyre, Shirley and Villette, Beulah,
Rutledge, The Mill on the Floss, Line Upon Line, Peep of
Day* and other titles; *Miss Leslie's New Cookery Book,* and
Youatt and Martin, *On Cattle.*

The North Carolina Mutual Life Insurance Company
then in its "tenth year of successful operation," announced
on June 13, 1861, in spite of the war, that it would insure
the lives of all healthy persons from fourteen to sixty years
of age, and in spite of the precarious nature of slave property, all slaves from ten to sixty years of age. It promised
to pay for all losses punctually "within 90 days."[21]

Some of these advertisements were of a serious nature,
patriotic, or devoted to the Confederate cause. Others were
light and humorous. A *Daily Bulletin* advertisement titled
"For the Volunteers," said the *Bulletin* desired to send "a
lot of potatoes, pickles, and light bread to the Hornets and
the Grays." It promised that any of these items left at the
Rock Island office by 4:00 P.M. Thursday would be forwarded.[22] M. E. Daye and Company advertised envelopes
in all colors "with the Southern Confederacy Flag on
them."[23] More realistic was Seth Jones whose advertisement

indicated that he lived at Pomona, fourteen miles northeast of Raleigh. His announcement was as follows:

BEST OLD APPLE and Peach Brandy, For Sale by the Barrel or Half Barrel, five years old at $2 per gallon.

Also Cows and young calves of the best breed—North Devon and Durham Shorthorn. Also 2 or 3 young bulls and several heifers of the same breed, from one to three years old. For terms apply to   SETH JONES[24]

The election of Lincoln affected the American economy, but how much it would be difficult to determine. All southern newspapers were neither pro-Confederate or pro-Union, and few of them were entirely neutral. However, newspapers and periodicals, in the North and in the South, indicated various effects of this election.

By the end of November these effects were being reported. On November 19, 20, and 21 the Virginia banks suspended specie payments. New York banks began discounting all bills on banks south of Washington, D. C. 20 to 25 per cent, those on Illinois and Wisconsin banks at 15 per cent and those on other Western and Canadian banks at 3 to 5 per cent on November 21. The New York money panic which was described as "equal to that of 1857," continued on November 22. On that date the Washington and Baltimore banks suspended specie payments and all of the banks of New York made common stock of their specie, without a determination to suspend, and discussed the policy of issuing 7 per cent script based on good collateral security. In the midst of this panic, a banner bearing the inscription "Southern Confederacy," with one star in the center was run up on Tuesday, November 27, on the Breckinridge pole in Raleigh. By the following day, large masses of workmen had been discharged from northern manufactories and large supplies of the most improved types of firearms had been shipped to Georgia and Alabama.[25]

On January 14, 1861, slaves were reported as selling in Richmond, Virginia, at from 40 to 50 per cent less than before the election.[26] On January 15, the Norfolk Day Book reported that slaves who had been hired for between $125 and $150 could be hired for $80 or $90, and that women who had been purchased for $80 were being sold for $50 and $60. These falling prices were reported to be in conformity with the depreciation of all kinds of property.[27] In Raleigh, a Negro woman whose age was forty sold on December 6, 1860, for $250, and a girl "who would have brought $1,000 a few months ago" sold for $505. The Raleigh report indicated that sales of slaves in Georgia, Richmond, and elsewhere were being made "at about the same rate." Reflecting the interest of a considerable non-slaveholding artisan class in North Carolina, the report summed up conditions as follows:

> . . . If dissolution should take place, likely negro men will not fetch $400, women much less . . . land and all other kinds of property will fall in proportion. The seceding States will open the African slave trade, countless numbers of wild barbarians will be brought over and sold in the South, to the great detriment of the owners of slaves in North Carolina. Free trade will follow. The labor of Europe will supplant the industry of the white mechanics of the South, and every mill and machine shop will have to close. There will be no mistake in this, for it is what the secessionists have contended for for the last thirty years. The hard working mechanics of the county—of the boasted South —are nothing in their vision,—but a *monopoly of the lands—* negroes—and free trade—to them is everything.

> Let the slaveholders, as well as the non-slaveholders in North Carolina be warned.[28]

The foregoing pessimistic views may not have been typical, because war activities usually increase rather than decrease economic activity. The economy may have been depressed immediately after the election, but a year later it seemed to have recovered from its worst effects. Many Negroes were employed and the abundance of money boosted prices, because economic activity had to go on in spite of the war. On November 25, 1861, John C. Moore auctioned slaves near Eagle Rock as follows: George, twenty-one years old, $1,245; Jim, eighteen, $755; Isaac, fifteen, $705; Catherine, twelve, $615; and "Woman Becky," twenty-four, with two children, one two and one four years old, $1,535. The average of more than $690 was considered "high prices for the times." They were taken to prove that there was an abundance of money in the pockets of the people of North Carolina and that slave property was as secure as it was prior to secession.[29] The fiscal report of the president of the Raleigh and Gaston Railroad for the fiscal year ending May 31, 1861, indicated that the railroad had a net profit of $128,113,92 and was operating at 40.30 per cent of receipts.[30] In December of that year, the Convention took action to halt speculation in the process of trade. In an ordinance which was to be in force only "during the present war," unless repealed or modified by the General Assembly, the Convention made speculation a misdemeanor and ruled that

whoever shall engross or get into his hands by buying, corn or other grain, pork or beef, . . . fish, salted or smoked, cheese, fish, coffee, sugar, tea, salt, saltpetre or other dead vituals whatever, and . . . leather, to the intent to sell the same again at unreasonable prices, or to keep the same from market, and prevent the same from passing into the hands and use of the people, or to any other intent than to his own use and consumption, or for sale at reasonable prices, or for charitable distribution amongst the poor and necessitous persons . . . upon conviction . . . or confession, shall be punished for a misdemeanor, and . . . required to enter into recognizance with sufficient surety for his good behavior for the space of three years, in such sum as the court may direct.[31]

Much of the trade involved providing basic clothing and equipment for the slaves. Some slaveholders were extremely careful to see that their slaves had shoes in the fall. Large quantities of cloth of uniform quality and color were purchased. Out of it, clothing for the slave families was made. As early as October 29, 1861, J. E. B. Grimes indicated that all of his slaves had shoes, with the exception of eight to whom he had given shoes the previous summer. In discussing the war with Major Byran Grimes, he also said that he thought his slaves' clothing was "about made up." With obvious reference to his probable rank, he said he would be willing "to go as anything" (any rank) that would "allow me a horse and a 'nigger,' " and that he would be obligated to have both. His conclusion seems to have been that he would not enter the service, because he said:

> . . . I can't stand it as a "private" and I see no chance of being either Capt. or Lieut Grimes I am afraid I am doomed to weigh cotton & whip negroes when shooting the damned abolitionists would be much more pleasant pastime.[32]

The people of North Carolina expected their friends to favor them in countless ways, but some commodities which the owner might have sold were given away. For example, Thomas Ruffin regularly gave mutton to his friends at Christmas time. Weldon N. Edwards of Popular Mount wrote Ruffin on October 1, 1860 to

> Say to Mr. Holt, if you please, that I want him to send me to Ridgeway, at the *earliest day*, seven pieces (7) of Cotton shirting for negroes—and (3) three pieces of striped or checked Cotton Cloth for negro women—the sample you had pleases Mrs. E., it is dark and suits her hands. . . . Tell him if *you don't pay him*, I will by check on Petersbg., or by sending the money.[33]

Fifteen days later, Edwards wrote Ruffin that he had received a bill from Holt for "the cloth you ordered for me." He expressed satisfaction that there was "one at Alamance" to whom he could send "little requests *sans ceremonie*," and requested that Ruffin give an enclosed $34.50 to Holt for him, adding that the sum was "too small for a check." The bale of cloth still had not arrived at Ridgeway.[34] Kenneth Raynor of Raleigh was writing to Ruffin on November 8 concerning an order for some "honey blade" millet seed, but his letter digressed into public affairs. He referred to Lincoln's election, expressed his alarm and the fear that South Carolina would secede and two or three other states would follow. Urging Judge Ruffin to write to Governor Ellis as to what should be the tone of his message to the General Assembly, he said there was still some uncertainty as to how Virginia had voted. Then he said: "I shall be pleased to receive the 'honey blade' millet seed from you."[35]

The plantation seemed to have been a busy place even during the winter. A plantation owner sometimes held several estates in various parts of the South and had to spend some time on all of them. Some descriptions of these operations are contained in a letter by Paul C. Cameron of Hillsboro to Ruffin, dated January 28, 1860, excerpts of which read as follows:

> I need 50 bushels of Simon Pure Winter Oats—free from Onion seed and all other impurities to seed my bottom land at this place. . . .

> I have had a letter from Mr. K. P. Battle in behalf of the Committee requesting me to deliver the address at the State Fair! To this I said No Sir—re Bob Jenkins. brick making, tobacco cutting, wheat seeding, don't allow the time for such affairs, besides I may have to go to N. Y. I must be on my place in Mississippi in the next 30 or 35 days, and I shall take with me a family of 40 slaves.[36]

The varied and complicated forms and usages involved in the commercial and domestic affairs of these people were executed with amazing legal precision. Causes frequently arose which involved devisees and decendants of devisees, citizens with judgments against devisors, spouses and their property rights, and husband-wife relations of a meaner sort.

Daniel Daughtertry [sic] of Craven County married Jane L. Davis, also of Craven, whose father was deceased. The marriage had taken place with the full consent of her mother and all of her immediate family. It was considered an eligible match, but the said *femme coverte* possessed only a small estate, principally land. Daughtertry ascertained that his wife was not quite fifteen at the time of their marriage, and since she had little property, applied to the General Assembly for relief. On January 31, 1861, the Assembly ratified "An Act for the Relief of Daniel Daughtertry." This law provided that Mrs. Daughtertry's interests would be greatly promoted by releasing her said husband of "the pains, penalties, disabilities, and forfeitures aforesaid," and that her husband be discharged and exempted from them under provisions of the *Revised Code*, Chapter LVIII, Section 10 and 11, incurred by reason of his marriage to the said Jane L. Davis before she reached the age of fifteen.[37]

Joseph Barber on August 5 and August 12, 1861, notified all persons not to harbor, trade with, or credit his wife, Helen, on his account "as she has left my bed and board without cause." While warning that he would not pay any debts contracted by her, he would treat her kindly if she would return, he said, and thereby notified her to come home, "where she would be amply provided for."[38] On December 23 of that year, Archibald C. Caldwell announced that all persons were forewarned against trading with or boarding his wife, Ann, formerly Ann Currie. He said he would not be responsible for any of her contracts, "she having left my bed and board without just cause."[39]

Terest Carman and her sister Mary Heath were joint owners of a valuable lot of slaves, dependent upon a life estate of Edmund Heath. The said slaves were valued at between ten thousand and twelve thousand dollars. Stephen Page who had sought several times to purchase Carman's interests in the slaves applied to her again in 1857 and informed her that he was owner of the interest that had belonged to Mary Heath. He offered her one thousand dollars for her interest but she refused to accept it. A few days later, Page called and informed her that he had been informed "by a gentleman of the bar" that there would be some doubt about the title to the remainder of these slaves after the death of Edmund Heath. He proposed they compromise with the children of the said Heath, whom Page alleged were claimants of the slaves and would bring suit for them.

Later after she became ill, the plaintiff alleged, and while she was prostrated by disease, she yielded to the defendant's entreaties and signed an indenture transferring the slaves to Page. Page did not even read the deed to her, she claimed. She was entirely ignorant of its contents, and the price mentioned in the deed was $1,110.

In a cause removed from the Court of Equity of Carteret County heard in the 1860 fall term of the North Carolina Supreme Court, Page answered that he had not importuned the plaintiff and alleged that the plaintiff, Terest Carman, on several occasions, sent for him and offered to sell her interest in the slaves at the price of $1,500. On the occasion when the deed was made, he said he "called on her by her request" and the terms of the deed were proposed by the defendant herself. The defendant agreed to pay $100 down, and the balance in one, two, three, four, and five years with good security and with interest. Such terms could be arranged, because Edmund Heath . . . "between seventy and eighty years of age, was of robust constitution, and was expected to have a long life."

The testimony was predominantly in favor of the defendant. The allegations of the will were, therefore, not sustained by proof, so the case was dismissed.[40] The plaintiff lost title to her slaves upon receipt of the price mentioned in the deed.

In an appeal made from an opinion of the fall, 1860, Court of Equity of Bladen County dissolving sequestration, William J. McNeill asked the State Supreme Court to review his case in its fall, 1860, term. The complainant was a son by a former husband of Mrs. Mary Bradley, wife of the defendant, William Bradley. Bradley had "separated himself from his wife" and had another woman living with him. He sold all of the property acquired by his marriage, except the slaves, subject of this action, and had no other property. He sought the advice of H. H. Robinson as to whether he could legally sell the slaves. Robinson intimated in indirect but intelligible terms that if Bradley could again gain possession of the slaves, he would put them beyond reach of the claimant.

The Supreme Court reversed the action of the lower court dissolving the sequestration proceedings and ordered them to proceed.[41]

Henry S. Lloyd, testator, heavily in debt, provided for the payment of his debts as follows:

> I authorize and empower my executors to carry on my farms for the term of two years after my decease, and to adopt all measures . . . , if the same be necessary, to pay debts, and to apply the income thereof . . . to the payment of my debts.

He made a further devise of his town property for the same purpose. Then he proceeded to "give and bequeath" to his aunt, Helen B. Slade: "all my negroes on my Roanoke plantation; and all my negroes on my Edgecombe farms, which I got from Martin County, whether I inherited or purchased them," with a residuary clause to his sisters and two brothers.

About 1850, the testator's grandmother, having died and

devised to him valuable farms in Edgecombe, the devisor moved from Martin County and established residence in Edgecombe County. He took with him several slaves and left twenty-seven slaves on his Roanoke plantation when he died in Philadelphia in January, 1860, all listed in the bill of the plaintiff. All of these slaves except Weaver, who was purchased in Richmond in 1856 and carried to the Roanoke plantation, were bequeathed to the testator in the original will of Henry Slade, maternal grandfather of Lloyd. There was a limitation over to his aunts, Helen B. Slade and Chloe Hinton, if he should die without issue.

There were thirty-five slaves brought from Roanoke plantation to Edgecombe, twenty-two of whom had been bequeathed to the devisor by Slade, or were decendants of such slaves. The remainder of them and their increase were purchased by the testator in various contiguous counties and taken to the Roanoke plantation. Two of these slaves were purchased in Martin County. Four of the slaves on the Edgecombe farms were offspring of the slaves moved from Martin to Edgecombe County, and born in Edgecombe.

Several questions were raised: whether the rights and interests of Helen Slade in the Roanoke plantation were subject to use according to the devise of the said Henry S. Lloyd to pay his debts; which slaves passed by the said devise to Helen Slade; and whether Sally, born of a woman given by Henry Slade to the devisor who belonged to the Roanoke plantation, lived among the defendant's slaves, and was so residing when the devisor died, passed by the granting clause.

The cause originated in the Court of Equity and Edgecombe County, was set down for hearing on the bill, answers, and exhibits and sent to the North Carolina Supreme Court by consent. It was titled *William Norfleet and D. P. Lloyd v. Helen B. Slade et al.*

The Supreme Court ruled: First, the testator intended that all of the plantations he worked be continued in cultivation two years for the payment of his debts, and as far as practical and consistent with the rights of others his will should be executed. Second, the court could not interfere as far as Mrs. Hinton was concerned. Since Miss Slade received a large estate under the will, she was bound to carry out, even to the prejudice of her own rights, the manifest purpose of the devisor in respect to his Roanoke plantation. Third, involved was a principle of equity which requires that a legatee who elects to take under the will must do so subject to all of the provisions of the instrument that affects his interests. Fourth, the bequest embraced all of the slaves at the time worked on the Roanoke plantation without regard to the source from which they were derived. Fifth, all of the slaves on the Edgecombe farms who had been removed from Martin County, "no matter how, or from what quarter derived," passed "under the bequest, also the slaves on the Edgecombe farms which had been brought in Martin." Sixth, "While the testator is making provision to restore the slaves to their original places of residence, and to their family connections, it would be an inconsistent and harsh construction to hold that he intended to separate infant children from their mothers. . . . It was intended the children should go with their mothers, and . . . they are embraced in the bequest of Miss Slade."[42]

Another case involving slave property was *Amelia Smith v. Leland Martin et al.,* a case moved from the Court of Equity of Wilkes County, decided in the fall, (December), 1860, term but reported in the spring (June), 1861, proceedings of the Supreme Court.

Robert Martin conveyed to his daughter, the plaintiff, a married woman suing by her next friend, a female slave, Dinah, who was "not to be at the disposal of Samuel P. Smith, her husband, in no manner whatsoever."

The supreme Court held that: First, where slaves were conveyed to a *femme coverte* by a deed of gift, and the first clause of the conveyance passed the legal estate to her and the heirs of her body, a subsequent clause of conveyance restraining her husband from all control over said slaves was inconsistent with the first clause and therefore inoperative, and the slaves vested in the husband's *jure mariti*. Second, in order to create a separate estate in a *femme coverte* there must be words sufficient to raise a trust for her benefit.[48]

North Carolina, like the rest of the South, possessed political, economic, educational, religious, and social institutions remarkably different from those outside the South. Its economic system was based on an ideology different from that in the North and the other institutions in this system were dominated by this strange ideology. The northerners who lived in the State apparently accepted the way of life in the South, but the reaction of the people was varied.

When the loyalty of W. Hurson Twichell, native of Connecticut, was questioned after the beginning of the war, he was held in confinement. Some of the citizens of Smithfield, Johnston County, petitioned the Governor to release him. They said Twichell and his family had lived for many years in that county, that he was a farmer, and that "his interests at home as a farmer" were "suffering much and must continue to suffer unless relieved by your excellency." His deportment "had won the confidence and esteem of the community," the petition continued and "we have no reason to believe that he sympathizes with the North in our present difficulties." It was not dated, but an endorsement was dated June 6.[70] Hough Downing wrote Governor John W. Ellis on June 19 that he had lived several years in North Carolina, but his family was in Philadelphia, Pennsylvania. Since he considered North Carolina "his future home," he told the Governor, he was requesting a "passport through the Confederate States not only to go north but also to return with my family."[71]

Some northerners were less well adjusted. S. S. Carter of Cartersville in Chatham County complained in April, 1861, that Henry T. Daggett, "a Yankee Bootmaker" came from South Weymouth, Massachusetts, "since the first of April, 1861, to work at the shoe business in Fayetteville" and had been working for Carter. He said a lady sent a gold watch and chain to him by Daggett who, "being an abolitionist and swindler, got scared at the secession cause" in Fayetteville. He pawned the gold watch which Carter valued at $145, for $26 in Raleigh. The *Fayetteville Observer* published an announcement demanding the watch from the Adams' Express Company on payment of the redemption money and forbade the party concerned to send the watch to Daggett in Boston. Carter in his advertisement expressed the hope that C. C. Barbee and Company, and P. Shemwell of Fayetteville would not send Daggett's trunk and gold watch which they had, but would "give me chance to pay the redemption money on said property," alleging that Daggett had "injured me at least $150." He promised to take the articles and "bind myself in the presence of any respectable parties to send them to him when he sends me the money I pay to redeem them."[72]

Chapter Three

State and Local Regulations

B Y 1861, the restrictions believed necessary to control the slaves who constituted one third of the total North Carolina population had been extended, consciously or unconsciously, to regulate the conduct of bound white servants and affected the lives of almost everyone in the state.

T. M. Scott of Greensboro wrote Thomas Ruffin as county attorney on May 3, 1860, informing Judge Ruffin that he had indicted some men in the county court for playing cards without betting. He remined the Judge that Ruffin, in a cause in which several men were charged with playing cards in a house "where spiritious liquors were sold" without betting, had charged the jury under provisions of Chapter XXXIV, Section 75, that playing cards in such places, even if there was no betting, was an indictable offense. Scott asked for information[1] which Ruffin provided when he acknowledged Scott's letter on June 2.[2]

A second example of the restrictions on the freedom of the North Carolina people is indicated by a writ issued by Judge R. M. Saunders "near the end of 1959" which ordered J. H. Moore "to take charge of a quantity of Helper's *Impending Crisis,* sent by express to High Point in this State, and arrest the consignee of said books." Moore petitioned the General Assembly on January 12, 1861, for the expense incurred in paying the freight on these books, which were publicly burned, and his time and traveling expenses which he reported amounted to about $10, which he had not been reimbursed. He said his bill was small but too much for him to lose, although not chargeable to any particular county.

The Committee on Claims to whom Moore's resolution was referred reported a new resolution to the House on February 20 and recommended "that it do pass." It authorized the public treasurer to pay Moore $10 out of any money in the treasury "not otherwise appropriated."[3]

A moderating force against terrorism was Benjamin S. Hendrick of 15 West Twenty-sixth Street, New York, former University of North Carolina chemistry professor. Dismissed in 1856 because of his belief in the principles of free soil, he wrote Thomas Ruffin a few weeks later to use his influence to arrest the terrorism and fanaticism which "so much disturbs the South." He said the laws should protect the people, but they do not know what their rights are under the law.

In order that Ruffin might know the offenses some of the men were accused of, he enclosed a copy of Helper's book in which he told Ruffin he would not find a word addressed to either slave or free Negroes. He asked Ruffin to examine it and see whether there was anything in it which one free man might not "properly address to another."[4]

When Rankin, a free Negro, was involved in an altercation in Salisbury on March 17, 1861 with another free Negro, P. M. Williams, a magistrate, remonstrated him. Rankin struck Williams with a stick and fled. He kept away those who pursued him with a knife, but when he was finally taken they proposed to hang him. When asked whether he prefered five hundred lashes or hanging, he chose the latter. The rope already around his neck, it was thrown over the limb of a tree and he was drawn up. Shortly afterwards some of the members of the lynch party ordered him cut down. He fell to his face, bleeding at the ears and nose.[5]

The second extra session of the Assembly amended Section 1 of Chapter XIV of the *Laws of North Carolina* to make Indians competent witnesses on September 13,[6] but the Convention repealed that chapter on December 6.[7] On the same day, the Convention amended the Fourth Article, Second Section of the State Constitution to read as follows:

> No person who shall deny the being of God or the divine authority of both the Old and the New Testaments, or shall hold religious opinions incompatible with the freedom or safety of the State, shall be capable of holding any office or place of trust or profit in the civil department of this State.[8]

The Convention thus excluded the Jews from public office but left them eligible to serve in the army or navy.

During the year beginning December 1, 1860, and ending November 30, 1861, more than twelve separate legislative proposals restricting the freedom of the people were introduced in the Assembly. From Currituck County came a proposal, dated December 4, 1860, requesting the Assembly to relieve that county of the free Negroes. They had at all times "free communication with the slaves," the petition reads, and were "a ready and safe medium for the diffusion of incendiary doctrines." The specific request was that the free colored population be expelled or reduced to slavery. Nathan N. Fleming introduced House Bill 19 to prevent emancipation of slaves by will on that same date. It passed the first reading and it was moved that it be postponed indefinitely, but the motion was lost 101 to 3. The vote to advance the bill to third reading was 102 to 5. It subsequently became Senate Bill 41 and on January 28, 1861, passed the third reading in the Senate and was ordered enrolled on January 29. A House message dated February 1 informed the Senate that the engrossed bill had been signed by the Speaker of the House. It was being transmitted for the signature of the Speaker of the Senate.[9] On Monday,

January 7, the Committee on the Judiciary received the following numbered bills: a bill regarding the hiring of slaves, a bill prohibiting trade with slaves, a bill "to regulate the free Negroes in the State," "a bill to permit free persons of color to select their own masters and become slaves," and a bill to bind out certain persons of color.[10] A second bill to prohibit emancipation of slaves by will was read a second time and passed in the Senate on January 8.[11]

Four undated proposals introduced during the period were designed to achieve the following purposes: first, to prevent Negroes from returning to North Carolina after leaving on the grounds that they were forced to leave; second, to prevent slaves from furnishing the means to free Negroes and white persons in the North to purchase their freedom; third, to prevent slaves from remaining in the State as property of freedmen but "really as free Negroes, to the evil example and great injury to our own slaves"; and fourth, to prevent free Negroes who had been out of the state more than ten days to return. Violators of the latter law were to forfeit their freedom, be enslaved, and ordered sold for cash to the highest bidder. The purchase price was to go to the informers and prosecutors, if there were any. If there were neither, one half of it was to go to the common school fund and the other half to the treasury of the state. When it was found that a slave had been acquired for the purpose of permitting him "to live and act as free," such transfers were to be declared null and void, the slave ordered sold for cash to the highest bidder as a slave for life, and the proceeds distributed as aforesaid. Another still more complete bill covering this subject was House Bill 249, introduced on January 10 and engrossed.[12]

A bill for the protection of stock provided that each family be permitted to have one dog for use and protection on the premises. If found running at large "without the owner's presence or control," the bill provided that it would be lawful for any person thus finding the animal "to destroy him as a nuisance." All dogs in excess of one were to be taxed one dollar, the revenue from the said tax to be held in the treasury to pay for losses sustained by loss of stock killed or injured by dogs. It was tabled in the Senate on February 21.[13]

A resolution introduced on June 10 provided that the North Carolina Constitution be amended to give the General Assembly full power to dispose of the free Negro population of the State, and that a committee of five be appointed to prepare an ordinance to execute these plans. Apparently no action was taken on it in the first extra session, but it was referred to the Committee on the Bill of Rights on November 21. A resolution to amend the Bill of Rights by substituting the words "white person" for "freeman" and to "inquire into the expediency and propriety of all other and necessary amendments to the Constitution affecting the colored population of this State," was also introduced on June 10 in the first extra session and referred to a select committee on November 25, in the second extra session of the Assembly.[14]

Obviously these restrictions were not entirely unbearable, but the fact that they could be tolerated was due largely to the consideration the Assembly was often ready to give individuals through special legislation. There seems to have been a penalty of double taxation for failure to list property. A resolution in favor of Jarvis Baxton prepared about August 27, 1861, however, was introduced in the Assembly to release him from the double tax penalty for which he appeared to be liable for failure to list his taxes for 1860. House Resolution 150 and Senate Bill 98 were prepared to exempt the State printer "and the hands in his employ" from military duty "during the sitting of the legislature."[15] The privilege of special legislation was extended to free Negroes and slaves, but what few rights they had deteriorated rapidly after the nomination of Abraham Lincoln.

As early as December 19, 1860, William T. Marsh of Beaufort moved that a message be sent to the Senate, proposing appointment of a joint committee of five members from each house "upon the subject of Slaves and Free Negroes." It was promptly adopted.[16] House Bill 388, an act to provide for the collection of taxes from insolvent free Negroes, followed shortly thereafter. It provided that free Negroes liable for taxes and without property after October 1 each year were to be reported by the sheriff "to the first county court held after said first day of October." The court was to direct the clerk to issue a *capias ad respondendum* for such tax. If the court found the defendant unable to pay the tax and costs, the sheriff was directed to "hire out said free negro publicly at the courthouse door during the term of the court or [as] soon thereafter as convenient to any person who would pay the said tax and costs or the greater part thereof for the service of said free negro for the shortest space of time, not exceeding two years. . . ." The power and authority of the person so hiring such insolvent free Negroes was to be the same as that held by masters over free Negro apprentices. The Committee on Slaves and Free Negroes recommended that it pass.[17]

As a result of restrictions on freedom and various proposals for additional restrictions on the conduct and activities of white and black persons, many of the free colored population considered it feasible to re-enslave themselves. This led to scores of petitions for special and general legislation on this subject. Ellen Ransom, "a free woman of color" of Franklin County, in order to "procure for herself a good and lasting home," petitioned the Assembly to pass an act allowing her to enslave herself to Leonidas Perry. It was signed in the presence of A. H. Green and Henry Sherrod and dated December 1, 1860. On December 6, B. F. Green witnessed and signed a paper in which she stated:

I shall apply to the present General Assembly to permit me to enter into slavery as the slave of Leonidas Perry, Esq [*sic*] of Franklin County.

A bill with these provisions was found among the papers.

A petition signed by the mark of Richard Garnes, his wife, Nancy, and their six children of Jones County on January 10, 1861, stated that they were desirous of becoming the slaves for life of Joseph A. Hartley, also of Jones County. They petitioned the Assembly "to pass any and all such laws as may be necessary to carry this object into effect." The petition was not witnessed and there were variations in the spelling of the family name.

Leah White of Jones County petitioned the Assembly on January 21 to enact legislation permitting her and her two small children to become slaves. She clearly indicated that she wished to choose her own master or mistress, and her petition was signed by four witnesses. The Committee on Propositions and Grievances to which it was referred sent the petition, which subsequently became Private House Bill 415, back to the House with the amendment that she select her master or mistress in open court and with the approbation of the Court of Pleas and Quarter Sessions for Jones County, and recommended that it pass.

A paper dated August 13 and signed by Elic Oliver and Julia, his wife, petitioned the Assembly to pass a law to permit him to become the slave of Dr. J. I. A. Beasley of Forsythe County. The Committee recommended that it not pass and on August 31 it was postponed indefinitely.

An undated petition by Nelson Patterson gave as his reason for wishing to be enslaved the belief that his social status would be improved by becoming a slave. He petitioned the Assembly for a law that would permit him to become a slave of the master of his wife.[18] Other reasons given for wishing to become slaves included "the present troubled state of the country" and a preference to remain "as slaves rather than to be set adrift to provide for oure selves [sic]." They sometimes indicated that they were "tired of, and dissatisfied" in their present condition and felt satisfied that they "would be more contented and happy as slaves."

The freedom of the free Negro was greatly restricted as indicated by the following petition by citizens of Alleghany County:

> We the undersigned Citizens of Alleghany County pray your honorable body to pass a law authorizing one Frances Raphel, a Free mulatto woman, now residing in Grayson County V.A. [sic] The rite [sic] to remove to Alleghany County N. C. She being the lawful wife of N. V. Raphel, who lives in Alleghany County and neither of them having The rite [sic] under the act of Assembly to remove across the State line and we as in duty bound will ever pray

It could not be ascertained what action was taken on the petition. House Bill 93 to permit Elizabeth Chavers, a "free Negro woman aged 26" and her infant child of Wake County to enslave herself and the child to Benjamin H. Graham for life was presented on September 13. The Committee on Propositions and Grievances reported it favorably but recommended that the child not be enslaved "beyond the age of twenty-one." When House Bill 278, an undated act to permit Francis Russel, a free Negro, to become an inhabitant of the state, was introduced, however, it was recommended that it not pass.[19]

Bills to permit free colored persons individually and collectively to become slaves were introduced in both houses. Since the main endeavor was to secure basic enabling legislation, the fact that these bills were not always numbered does not present a serious problem. E. J. Blount of Pitt County introduced a bill on January 10 to permit John Conner, a free man of color, to become a slave. It was read the first time, passed, and referred to the Committee on Propositions and Grievances.[20] House Bill 457 to permit Negroes to select their masters and become slaves was returned from the Committee on Slaves and Free Negroes on February 7, with the recommendation that it pass. The House passed an engrossed bill on February 22 and asked Senate concurrence in a message signed by W. T. Dortch, Secretary of the House of Commons, To Henry T. Clark, Speaker of the Senate. Another similar bill was passed by the House and sent to the Senate by Dortch in the second extra session of the Assembly on September 7.[21] House Bill 162, to allow John Phillips to enslave himself, and House Bill 163, to allow Janett Wright to enslave herself, passed the third reading in the House on September 11 and were ordered engrossed.[22] Finally House Bill 168, Senate Bill 116, to authorize Negroes to go into voluntary servitude were reported unfavorably and laid on the table.[23]

Three additional general bills and five special bills were also found. The fact that the Assembly was unwilling to approve legislation permitting free Negroes to enslave themselves is attested by the fact that the committees frequently recommended that these bills not pass. There was a struggle in the Assembly throughout much of the 1860-61 session and extra sessions of the Assembly, but no such legislation was ever passed.

As a result of the conditions in 1860 and 1861, most of the legislation involving slaves and free Negroes was the result of requests for further restrictions on freedom and laws resulting from requests for re-enslavement of the free Negro population in the state.

Apparently few, if any, of these free colored people could write. Not only might it be expected that these petitions were written and sponsored by white persons, but some of them may be contemporary accounts prepared by unscrupulous persons concerned with a reinterpretation of the history of antebellum North Carolina. Furthermore, if the slave status was so desirable, why were so many restraints employed to control these slaves and prevent them from escaping?

The first major piece of legislation further regulating the activities of slaves and free Negroes was ratified on January 31, 1861. This law provided that no slave be emancipated by last will and testament, deed, or other instrument or conveyance to take effect after the death of the testator. Slaves "so attempted to be emancipated" were not to pass under any general residuary clause in any last will and testament, because in such case the testator would be considered to have died intestate.[24]

Both slaves and free Negroes were prohibited from wearing, carrying or keeping in their houses any shotgun, musket, rifle, pistol, sword, sword cane, dagger, bowie knife, powder, or shot. Persons who violated this law, one of four major pieces of legislation applied to slaves and free Negroes passed on February 23, were fined $50.[25] Publication or circulation of pamphlets or papers, handwritten or printed, in or out of North Carolina, which would tend to cause slaves to become discontent with bondage and free Negroes dissatisfied with their social condition was considered a felony. The penalty for this felony was death. Inflammatory language which would tend to incite in any slave or free Negro a spirit of insurrection, conspiracy, or rebellion was to be a misdemeanor, punishable by fine or imprisonment, at the discretion of the court.[26] On May 11, this law was amended to provide that any person who should "advise or conspire with a slave to rebel or make insurrection" in this State or with any person "to induce a slave to make insurrection," upon conviction, was to suffer death. The death penalty was required "whether such rebellion or insurrection be made or not."[27] The rules of evidence in indictments for trading with slaves were amended to read as follows:

. . . in all indictments for trading and trafficking [*sic*] with slaves, or for giving or selling liquor to slaves, wherein it is negatively to aver the consent of the owner or manager of the slave to the trading, selling, or giving, . . . the burden of proof shall rest upon the defendant to show that he had a written license or permit, as required by law, to trade, or give, or sell to the slave.[28]

Free Negroes were prohibited from purchasing or hiring "any slave or slaves or to have any slave or slaves bound as apprentices . . . or in any other wise to have the control, management, or services of any slave or slaves. . . ." The penalty was one hundred dollars for each offense, but was not to apply to colored persons who were in legal possession of slaves at the time the act was passed.[29] The second extra session of the Assembly amended the laws to make it illegal for any captain or other military official in the state to enroll any free Negroes, except for musicians, cooks, and washers. In time of actual service four cooks were to be employed in each company and be rationed and paid by the State. Four free Negroes were to be employed by each company as washers and rationed by the State but paid by the men of the company for whom they washed.

The Assembly and Convention were separate legislative bodies, each with full power to make laws, and each recognizing the right of the other to repeal laws made by the other body. The latter apparently agreed with the Assembly in its action in prohibiting emancipation of slaves by will, ratified on January 31, and the acts prohibiting free Negroes from having arms, and sale or gift of liquor to slaves without license. However, the Convention repealed the act of the Assembly which would have convened the Assembly on June 25. An ordinance ratified on June 19 provided that the act of the Assembly "is hereby abrogated and annulled" and that "there shall be a session of the General Assembly which shall convene on the 15th day of August next." The

Assembly amended the law to make Indians witnesses in the second extra session, 1861, but the Convention repealed that law on December 6. The Assembly act permitting members of the Jewish faith to hold office was also repealed on December 6.[30]

The restrictions imposed on the freedom of the people of North Carolina were sometimes supplemented by city ordinances. In June, 1861, T. Williams, Clerk of Commissioners, and E. B. Jennings, Magistrate of Police of the Town of Shelby, announced a sweeping town ordinance, regulating the conduct of practically every person in the town. The citizens were prohibited from permitting any goat to run at large under penalty of five dollars. Occupants of houses within the town were required to keep them closed "so as to prevent hogs from lying under such houses, under penalty of one dollar for each week such house may be left in condition for hogs to lie under same." Persons who might get drunk and disturb "the quiet of citizens" were to be taken into custody by the town constable and "kept confined in a calaboose, or some place of confinement, until he becomes quiet and peaceful and pay a fine of one dollar." Persons who might retail tobacco not grown or manufactured in the county, on the square, streets, or alleys of Shelby were required to pay a tax of two dollars for each day of such retailing. The sale of less than one half of a box of tobacco was to be considered retailing. No person was to hitch or tie any horse, mare, or mule to the enclosure around the public square, "nor any shade tree on the square or in any of the public streets or alley's [sic], under penalty of one dollar." Persons with pools, vats, or ponds of water within the town were required to keep them cleared of stagnant water to prevent mosquitoes, under penalty of one dollar.

Negroes or free persons of color were not permitted "to suffer any slave to visit or to remain" in their house at night or on Sunday, under penalty of two dollars. Free colored persons who visited slaves in their own house or the house of their owners at night or Sunday were to be fined two dollars. Any free Negro "bedding or cohabiting with any slaves" was to be fined two dollars. The fine for violating the state law prohibiting free Negroes from having arms or weapons of any kind was five dollars. For gambling with slaves, also prohibited under the law, the municipal fine was five dollars, but the town commissioners might also order the defendant whipped "not exceeding thirty-nine lashes." The penalty for selling wine or spiritous liquors within the corporate limits of Shelby "of the measure of one quart or less" was twenty-five dollars.

"If any person shall own and suffer any proud slut to go loose within the incorporation," the law reads, "he or she shall pay a fine of two dollars. . . . And it shall be lawful for anyone to kill any proud slut which may be found loose . . . after the owner has knowledge that such is at large within in the corporate limits of the town."[31]

John I. Shaver, "intendent of the Town of Salisbury," announced on May 3 . . . "that the Town Patrol of Salisbury have discretionary powers to arrest and lock up in the calaboose any person, white or black, who may be found in the streets of Salisbury after dark who shall be guilty of any disorderly conduct or be able to give a satisfactory account of himself. . . ." Any person so committed was to be carried before Shaver "for further proceedings" on the following morning.[32]

Most of the legislation was designed to control slaves, free Negroes, and the more despicable white persons as indicated by such expressions as "discretionary powers to arrest" and "or be able to give a satisfactory account of himself" and the fact that one of the Salisbury laws was to be enforced only after dark.

The results of these conditions were expressed partly in terms of poverty and insecurity. The letters of Thomas

Ruffin afford some insight into the conditions of the people as well as the esteem in which he was held. On March 8, 1860, George B. Johnston of Chapel Hill wrote to Ruffin, asking Judge Ruffin to recommend him for a teaching position at the University of North Carolina. Because his letter is an indication of what must have been the chief consideration of the president in making faculty appointments, it is quoted below:

> Dr. and Respected Sir,
>   I make bold to intrude myself upon you, and ask your assistance in a matter of much interest to me; may I not hope that the intercourse always existing between our families and your intimate relation to some with whom I am connected, will in a measure excuse me. I am here, seeking a situation as tutor in the Faculty of our University; I have the *expressed* preference of the professor in whose department the vacancy occurs, and feel assured that I could secure the appointment if any person of your influence and character would take enough interest in my success to recommend me to the Faculty, or rather to the President individually. If . . . you are unwilling to do this, could I hope to get a letter from you to some such person as Gov. Graham or Gov. Manly with a view to making a similar request? . . .[33]

W. R. Richardson, a member of the staff of the North Carolina Treasury Department, wrote Ruffin on October 22, 1861, requesting that he offer "as soon as convenient" at the approaching session of the Convention, a resolution that "in view of the increased duties of his office, the chief clerk of the State Treasury Department shall hereafter receive an annual salary of twelve hundred dollars." He listed the addition of four specific new duties and a general increase in the business of the office as his reason for requesting the higher salary.[34] On November 25, Richardson wrote to Ruffin again, requesting that he take the subject of his salary increase before the Committee on Finance at its next meeting. "By so doing," he said, "you will confer a favor which I can not forget."[35]

Thomas Carter of Raleigh wrote Ruffin on December 3 that he was known "in this community as an energetic business man of first quality, competent to perform anything I undertake." Since his business was not "yielding support for my family," however, he said he "would be glad to receive the appointment of Commissioner of the Salt-Works or any other appointment the Convention can bestow." He said he had no doubt that Rayner Battle "and many other members of the Convention" would support his nomination.[36] J. W. Hall of Salisbury wrote on December 4 reminding Ruffin that the Confederate government had established a prison there for federal prisoners and that his name had been presented "as surgeon." He asked Ruffin and various others to write letters in his behalf.[37]

Some of these letters reflected the fearful, distressing nature of conditions even from the beginning. On September 10, 1860, Paul C. Cameron of Hillsboro wrote to Ruffin informing him that he had heard of the extensive illness of slaves in Ruffin's family. He referred to Weldon N. Edwards, Popular Mount slaveholder, whose tobacco barn in which his slaves had taken shelter from a storm, had blown down. Two of Edwards' slaves, one a carpenter, were taken out dead.[38] Edwards conceived of the federal government of the United States as already a failure, because on November 23 he wrote to Ruffin as follows:

. . . My mind is employed almost day and night upon the wretched condition of our country. It mortifies me to think that Govt. [sic] (federal) is a failure—the state Govts. are not yet. Both, however, rest on the same basis—the capacity of the constituent body for self government. The latter upon the will of the people—the former upon the will of the States.[39]

Charles Manly, former governor of North Carolina, wrote on January 16, 1861:

> My Dear Ch. Justice
> . . . Well, our country is destroyed forever! No reconstruction of the whole nor partial organizations will be worth a button. There can be no confidence in its stability or integrity, without credit at home or abroad, this great nation which yesterday was the glory of its citizens and the admiration of the world has in 90 days sunk down to ruin and contempt by the mechanizations of the devil and bankrupt politicians.[40]

W. C. Kerr of Davidson College told Ruffin on January 20 that he had been informed that Ruffin had a number of cases of diptheria in his black family and had been very successful in treating it with some simple remedies. He said that dreadful disease had appeared "in our midst" and requested that Ruffin inform him what treatment he used, "if the statement above is correct." He indicated that this information would also be useful to others.[41] William K. Ruffin wrote to Judge Ruffin from his home in Alamance County on February 18 while he was in Raleigh as a member of the Convention. Informing Ruffin that Cameron had suddenly been called to his Mississippi plantation, he said Cameron had been informed by telegraph that two of the slaves he had leased the previous fall had attempted to kill the overseer.[42]

Of less serious nature was a letter from Jeremiah Holt of Alamance County dated July 28. Holt said he had been informed by "my boy Thomas" that "he wants your Negro girl, Emily, for a wife if it is agreeable with you and wants a recommendation." Holt said that Thomas was a boy of good character, sober and honest, and permitted to pass and repass to Ruffin's house and home Monday morning on good behavior.[43]

Thus for these men, determined to maintain the status quo, life meant toil and trouble. We have noted certain restrictions, both State and local, and some possible results of these restrictions on the personal freedom of the people of North Carolina. Throughout this period, however, there was some concern about personal rights.

Jonathan Worth wrote the Rev. George McNeill, Jr., editor of the *North Carolina Presbyterian,* from Ashboro on March 10, 1860, in defense of the Rev. Daniel Worth who was awaiting trial on March 26 for his abolition activities. Worth listed various reasons why he believed the State should move cautiously in disposing of the case. He said the Rev. Mr. Worth was a minister and sixty-eight years of age. Harsh treatment would be excellent propaganda for the abolitionists because of his talent and exemplary morals. There was fear that punishment would make Worth a martyr, fear of the comments of the anti-slavery journals in the North, and the fear expressed by his defender that punishment would violate "Section 16 of the statute titled 'Crimes and Punishment.'" He expressed the fear that the law would "be enforced with the utmost rigor," while it seemed "to be most wise" to avoid whipping the prisoner on condition that he leave the State. "Let him be convicted," Worth added, "but in consideration of his age and being a minister of the gospel, let judgment be suspended on his entering into a recognizance for his good behavior."

Worth explained that he knew of only one man in the state who could "advise prudence and lenity in this matter and whose advise would be adopted without censure or suspicion as to his motives—and that man is Judge Ruffin— and my object in addressing you is to get you to call his attention to it."[44]

McNeill wrote Ruffin on March 12 that "the best thing I can do with the enclosed letter is to send it to you." He said that if Worth were convicted, he would publish an appeal to the governor to pardon him or remit the whipping—on condition that he leave the state forever. "In view of the fact that the *Presbyterian* was the first paper in the country to call attention to Worth's movement in N. C. [*sic*] and followed it up till [*sic*] he was arrested," the letter explained, "there will be no impropriety in this course. But if you advise the contrary it will not be done."[45]

In January, 1861, Governor Ellis issued a proclamation of a reward of four hundred dollars for the arrest and delivery to the sheriff of Northampton County of Ephraim, a slave charged with murdering Lucius Woodruff. Evans Ferguson and Ben Smith, free Negroes, arrested Ephraim and held him until "many citizens of the county took possession of him." They did not actually deliver the slave to the sheriff, but a bill was introduced in the Assembly "authorizing and instructing the Governor" to pay them the four hundred dollars out of any money in the Treasury not otherwise appropriated.

The House passed House Bill 411 to accomplish this purpose and sent it to the Senate on February 1, asking concurrence. The house bill was lost, but a subsequent bill was ratified on February 18, providing that the governor was authorized to pay these men the four-hundred-dollar reward.

Senate Bill 121, a bill to repeal the act passed by the 1860-61 Assembly prohibiting free Negroes from having arms, passed the second reading in the Senate on September 19, but the Senate Committee recommended that it not pass and it was lost.[46]

The *Western Sentinel* reported on June 3 that it understood that some of the free Negroes in the community were alarmed about their personal safety, but that this alarm was "altogether unfounded." The *Sentinel* expressed the belief that no free Negro who conducted himself properly would suffer any harm. It suggested that the free Negroes there do "as their brethren did at Newbern [*sic*]—volunteer to work in the cause of the State . . ." on forts, magazines, and other similar work.[47]

Among the other actions in the interest of personal rights, a bill was introduced in the House on September 11, providing for abolition of imprisonment for debt.[48]

The special legislation in favor of Ferguson and Smith may have been motivated by the desperate effort to protect slave property and maintain the institution of slavery. Special legislation itself was an evil, because it was sometimes employed to clear convicted persons of crime, yet the act would still be effective. North Carolina seems to have always been motivated by a sense of justice, but this sense of justice was always warped and twisted by the almost universal notion of subordination-superordination prevalent even in our time. Whatever the motivation for this concern about the condition of terror and insecurity, the Committee on the Declaration of Rights reported on December 10, 1861, that alteration of the "declaration of rights" affecting the existing constitutional rights and privileges of free Negroes "is unnecessary, inexpedient, and improper, and ought not to be made."[49]

Chapter Four

Education and Propaganda

LTHOUGH North Carolina was the first State in the Union to provide for higher education, having established the University of North Carolina in 1789, it was greatly handicapped most of the time prior to the Civil War by poverty, falling population, poor common schools, and poorly prepared and poorly paid teachers. Its declining population was indicated by the fact that it was authorized five representatives to the Congress of the United States in 1789, ten after the first census was tabulated in 1792, and thirteen in 1812, but due to population declines between 1812 and 1865 was entitled to only seven representatives at the end of the war. The influence of poor schools with low standards and poorly prepared teachers will be indicated later in this report.

Various types of persons, Harvard University graduates, "members of the Protestant Episcopal Church," and candidates for holy orders, sought teaching positions; however, their references were not to academic records but to high ranking churchmen and politicians.

S. S. Donaldson of Columbus, Georgia, offered his services as a teacher in North Carolina on July 25, 1860. He said he was a southern graduate of Harvard University seeking a position as private tutor or as teacher in a small school. His references were: the Honorable C. C. Clay, Jr., and the Honorable J. A. Pearce of the United States Senate; the Honorable W. H. Hillard of Montgomery, Alabama; the

Honorable M. J. Crawford, the Rev. W. N. Hawks, and
R. Carter, Esq., of Columbus, Georgia; and J. R. Jones, Esq.,
in whose family in Columbus Donaldson had taught since
April, 1858, and to whose address correspondence was to be
directed. From Havana, New York, a man advertising in
North Carolina as "A. M." said he was a graduate of Hobart
College and a candidate for Holy Orders and was seeking a
situation in some southern institution as a teacher of languages or in a family as a private tutor. His advertisement,
dated August 9, 1860, listed no references but indicated
that satisfactory references could be given.[1] When George A.
Selby of Lake Landing in Hyde County advertised for "a
lady to take charge of a family school" on September 13, he
specified that she must be competent to teach the usual
branches of English and music and that the annual salary
would be three hundred dollars, with board.[2] The Reverend
J. C. Huske of Fayetteville advertised on August 2, 1861,
that "a Southern Lady, a member of the Protestant Episcopal
Church," was seeking a position in a school or family. She
was offered as "competent to teach the usual English branches, French, and music," but although she was advertising
in a Fayetteville newspaper, she preferred "a situation in
Alabama or Mississippi."[3]

That the academies and colleges were small is attested by
the large number of these associations organized and operated for the first time during 1860 and 1861. Taking into
consideration the small population of North Carolina in
1861 and the minute proportion enrolled in any kind of
school, one might wonder whether there were any established academies and colleges prior to this period.

Judson Female College in the Town of Hendersonville,
incorporated on February 11, 1861, was authorized to "have
a perpetual succession and a common seal and to hold real
and personal property not to exceed three hundred thousand
dollars." The estate was to be controlled by the trustees

for "the use and purposes of the Baptist Church in North Carolina." Immediately it was authorized to confer such degrees or marks of distinction as were usually conferred by colleges and universities.[4] The charter for Mars Hill College had been issued in the 1858-59 session of the General Assembly. It provided for not less than thirty-one nor more than forty trustees, vacancies to be filled by the Western North Carolina Baptist Convention. Its real estate holdings were not to exceed fifty thousand dollars in value. The Assembly must have felt that the students, coeds *et al.*, were willing to walk a long way for liquor, because manufacture or sale of spirituous liquors or wines was not lawful within four miles of the College.[5] Yadkin Institute, which later became Yadkin College in 1861, was located in Davidson County. Chartered under the authority of an 1860-61 session law, it was authorized to go into operation as "soon as the trustees shall meet together and elect a president of the board of trustees—a majority of them being present—and accept this charter, unless the same shall be rejected by the Methodist Protestant Conference at its first session after its adoption by the board of trustees." The president and professors, "by and with consent of the trustees," were granted the power to confer such degrees or marks of literary distinction "as are usually conferred by colleges or universities."[6] Six academies, Bellevue Academy in Beaufort County, Hillsboro Military Academy in Orange County, Jefferson Academy in Ashe County, Oak Hill Military Academy and Tally Ho Female Academy in Granville County, and Richlands Institute in Haywood County, were chartered between February 18 and February 25, 1861.[7]

The Union Meeting of the Disciples of Christ, in conference at Trunters Creek in Beaufort County on "Friday before the 5th Lord's day in January," 1860, made extensive plans for the operation of the Kinston Female Academy.

Occupying "the best school room in the village, large enough to accomodate fifty or sixty pupils," the first session of the school had already opened on January 16. The minutes of the meeting indicated that the enrollment was not large, but the Union hoped to have "a full school" before that session closed.

The Union said that the school was designed as a permanent association and that it hoped to merit and receive the patronage of a "liberal, enlightened, and generous public." Its object was to impart a thorough knowledge of all of the branches taught. Pupils were not to be permitted "to pass over any study without understanding it, as is the case in many primary and even higher institutions of learning." The minutes then explained the curriculum of the school as follows:

> . . . Many unsuspecting persons are led away by high sounding names and hence desire to send their children to some institution called a College or Collegiate Institute. Such institutions have multiplied in North Carolina until almost every Rail-Road Depot is dignified with a College. But what advantages are gained by these pupils by patronizing them to the neglect of schools with less imposing names? None, absolutely none. They are often hurried through the *course* and come out very superficial graduates. . . .

> The course adopted by us embraces the *solid,* the *useful,* and the *ornamental.* We have not yet perfected our arrangements; but we hope by the beginning of the 2nd session (. . . about the middle of August), to get fully under way.

The curriculum consisted of "Higher English branches, embracing Grammar," geography, arithmetic, "natural, moral, and mental philosophy," chemistry, geology, etc., French, Latin, Greek, music, "together with all the Ornamental branches."

In pointing out the basic differences between the Kinston school and others, the announcement stressed the fact that the season was "full five calendar months. Listing in detail additional plans of the school, the announcement reads:

> . . . We are satisfied . . . by experience and observation that pupils advance more rapidly and are conducted much more easily, under a male superintendent than when under the sole management of a female. . . .
>
> We intend that our terms shall be *lower* than any other school offering similar inducements or equal advantages. Our contingent expenses will never exceed $1 . . . , charged when parents enter four or more pupils. . . . And now we make the following liberal offer to any young lady who may wish to qualify herself to teach: We will receive FIVE such young ladies, and *trust* them for their tuition, provided they can pay their board. . . . Our object is to do good in everything to which we devote our attention, and we hope the above proposition will be responded to by that number of ladies.
>
> The pupils are not annoyed by the effacious pertness of servants, nor by any domestic difficulties, broils, or quarrels . . . neither do we charge enough under the head of *contingent* or extra expenses, to pay for all the wood consumed in parlor, chamber, and kitchen.[8]

On April 15, Dr. John T. Walsh, Principal of the Kinston school, then referred to as the Kinston Female Seminary, announced the second session which was to begin July 23 and end on December 21. Tuition varied according to the grade level of instruction, as follows: elementary subjects or spelling, reading, writing, primary geography, and arithmetic, eight dollars; higher English or grammar, geography, arithmetic, history, geology, natural philosophy, and chemistry, ten dollars; higher English, including moral and mental philosophy, logic, rhetoric, algebra, and astronomy, twelve dollars; the languages, French, Latin, and Greek, fifteen dollars; and music, on piano, with use of instrument, seventeen dollars, or on melodeon, with use of instrument, twelve dollars. No deductions were to be made "except in cases of protracted illness."

Pupils could enter at any time and be charged from the time of entrance, but it was desirable that they should begin with the session. A few "small boys, of good character" would be taken under the special care of the principal when parents had both boys and girls and wished to enroll the boys; but whenever boys were enrolled, the parents were expected to enroll the girls also. If the girls were sent to other schools in Kinston, the boys were rejected.[9]

On June 22, the Right Reverend Thomas Atkinson, visitor, the Reverend Aldert Smedes, rector, and the Reverend Fred Fitzgerald, assistant, of St. Mary's School in Raleigh announced that the thirty-seventh term of the school would begin on July 6, but directed those interested to write to the rector for details. Jarvis Buxton, Rector of the Ravenscroft School in Asheville, announced on August 30 that "young men and young boys" were being received and that the tuition cost and board for ten months was one hundred fifty dollars. Half of this sum was to be paid in advance.[10]

Duncan McArthur's announcement on March 23, 1861, was unique in that it was more detailed and gave several references. He announced that "the undersigned" or references would "commence a School on the F. & W. Plank Road, nine miles from Fayetteville, three miles from Manchester P. O., and within half a mile of the Western Rail Road" on Monday, April 22. He proposed to give "universal attention to the school" and teach as thoroughly as was practicable.

Instruction was to be offered in orthography, reading, writing, arithmetic, geography, English, grammar, surveying, and geometry, use of logarithms, trigonometry, "area of land computed by difference of latitude and departure and also by various methods of plotting," astronomy, calculation, and projection, solar and lunar eclipses, and navigation.

Tuition, board, laundry, mending, lights, and bed and bedding were provided for thirty dollars per term of ten weeks. The references were: the Honorable J. G. Shepard, Dr. W. C. McDuffie, Joseph Arey, Esq., Sampson Boon, Esq., Colonel John McRae, Fayetteville, Dr. H. A. Bizzell, Clinton, William D. Smith, Wilmington, James M. Smith, Esq., David G. McDuffie, engineer and surveyor of Cumberland County, John C. Williams, Esq., and his son, Dr. J. C. Williams, of Harnett County.[11]

T. M. Jones of Greensboro Female College announced on July 20 that the fall, 1861 term would open "on the last Thursday in July." Board was fifty dollars and tuition was twenty dollars per session. Extra studies could be pursued "at reasonable rates." He said it was desirable that the pupils be present at the beginning of the session and that a catalogue containing complete information could be secured by writing directly to him.[12]

Donaldson Academy was more precise. Jessie R. McLean, principal of the Fayetteville school, placed the following announcement in the local newspaper on August 19:

SCHOOL NOTICE

My School, in the Donaldson Academy on Haymount, will be reopened on Tuesday, October 1st, 1861.

Terms Per Quarter of 10 Weeks:

English,	$7.50
Classical	10.00
Contingent	.25[13]

Private education in North Carolina was thus characterized by a large number of poor schools, poorly equipped, and necessarily with low standards. Many of them consisted of little more than an idea, a board of trustees, and the four bare walls of a building.

By 1861, the public school system had been organized more than thirty-five years. The common schools were headed by a State superintendent of common schools elected by the General Assembly, and superintendents of the county school units. Calvin H. Wiley was nominated by the Senate to fill this position on November 28, 1860. The committee appointed to superintend the election reported on that date that one hundred forty-nine votes had been counted and that one hundred forty-seven had been cast in favor of Wiley in the joint House and Senate election and that he was duly elected.[14]

Wiley's position was more like that of a chief clerk with little assistance. It resembled a position as working secretary of education, because the process of selecting the teachers and the administration were decentralized and the schools were not standardized.

William H. Brown announced on March 1, 1861, that the examining committee would meet at the Orange County courthouse in the Town of Hillsborough [sic] to examine persons who wished to teach in the common schools. Male applicants were to be examined on May 4, and on May 11 female applicants were to be examined. All who wished to obtain certificates to teach were required to attend these public examinations because no private examinations were to be given.[15] H. F. Byerly announced on July 12 that all persons who wished to secure a license to teach in the common schools of Forsythe County could meet at the courthouse in Winston on the last Saturday in July, the second Saturday in August, and Friday before the last Saturday in August, to be examined.[16] An announcement signed by the whole committee for Harnett County, dated August 5, was as follows:

> The Undersigned Committee of Examination for Harnett County will attend at Summerville on Thursday and Friday of Superior Court, (15th and 16th August) for the purpose of examining into the mental and moral qualifications of those wishing to teach Common Schools in said County.[17]

Not only were the common schools of North Carolina poorly organized, they were also poorly supported. Besides, there was a small but carefully organized movement underway in the State to cut off what little support the schools were already receiving through taxation. House Bill 173 to amend Chapter CII of the *Revised Code* which regulated salaries and fees, was introduced by S. H. Cannady on December 13, 1860. Designed to reduce the salary of the State Superintendent of Common Schools from $1,500 to $1,000, the proposed legislation would have become effective on January 1, 1861, just eighteen days later, but the House Committee on Education recommended that it not pass.[18] Senate Bill 173 to reduce the salary of the Superintendent of Common Schools was introduced but failed in the House 50 to 46 on February 16.[19] A bill was introduced in the first extra session of the 1860-61 Assembly designed to suspend the semi-annual distribution of funds for the common schools. The fund was to be paid to the public treasury to be used as other public money and the office of State superintendent of common schools was to be abolished. A bill to prevent collection of the school tax for the duration of the war, Senate Bill 19, introduced in second extra session of the 1860-61 Assembly, passed the third reading on September 19 and was engrossed.[20]

As a result of these efforts, so much of Chapter CX, Section 40 of the *Revised Code* as titled roads, ferries and bridges and exempted justices of the peace, constables, wardens of the poor, patrollers, and teachers and superintendents of common schools from working on the public roads of North Carolina, was repealed on August 4, 1861.[21] An act to prevent the collection of taxes for common school purposes was also ratified, though during the last three days of the second extra session of the Assembly. It provided that Chapter LXVI, Section 32 of the *Revised Code* of North Carolina which required county courts to lay and collect a tax for common school purposes, be repealed. However, to counties in which the justices, a majority being present, should "elect to lay such tax" it should not apply.[22]

In his plea for the common schools, Wiley said North Carolina had a large number of worthy people "in moderate circumstances," farmers, day laborers, mechanics, teachers, clerks, and professional and learned persons, who were greatly interested in a general system of cheap and efficient instruction. If they should migrate for lack of these facilities, he said, they would be difficult to replace.

"The non-slaveholders now among us," he continued, "born and educated in the South, connected by ties of blood and affinity with the owners of slaves, are . . . familiar with the character of Southern society, are . . . as conservative as any other." If they should leave the state, Wiley pleaded, "their place may be supplied by others raised under different systems, or educated for different prejudices and sympathies."

He believed education doubly necessary "in a society with African slavery," and that education would deter the most dangerous element of society in such States. He said efforts were being made "to get rid of . . . persons" who sink from the level of their society "to the free associations of the colored community, bound and free." They were not "safe members of society in slaveholding communities," Wiley said, because persons "abandoned to the instincts of a viscous nature do not sink to a place by themselves," because when they fall "from the stratum of decent white society, they sink into the bosom of another . . . community where their influence is necessarily evil and dangerous."

He denied that the presence of slaves retarded the "progress of civilization of the ruling race" and dismissed the charge as "inconsistent with the claim which anti-slavery leaders make for social and political equality of slave and master."

According to the southern notion that slavery tended to improve the slave, Wiley said that the slave's position was "highly educational" and that the master should be subjected to influences equally stimulating to him. The Negro slave in the United States was in a situation which furnished him "the most effectual appliances for the rapid improvement of a nature like his," Wiley said, and "born in a school the most completely adopted to his wants and capacity, and . . . under training every hour of his life."

Wiley was determined to do all that he could to preserve social distinctions between all white persons and all Negroes and equally determined that political equality not be permitted. He was determined, and enlisted the aid of the white population to "see that our part of the community preserve its relative position, and . . . be constantly . . . alert to prevent the sinking of any portion of the upper into the lower stratum of society." There this upper stratum "would become a source of demoralization to the lower stratum" or the African element of the population, referred to as the slaves and free Negroes, a reflection of the progress of the white man, and a source of constant danger "to the peace and order of the Commonwealth."[23]

Although taxation for the support of the common schools was discontinued in 1861, the effects of this action were not felt until the following year. In fall, 1861 appropriation for the schools was approximately $27 higher than the appropriation made the year before.

The fall, 1860, distribution of the State School Fund was $90,452.04—the same as the spring distribution. Alleghany, Madison, and Polk Counties were to receive their apportionments from the counties from which they were formed. Jackson County was to receive 30 per cent of the Macon County allotment and the balance of its share from the Haywood County allotment. The county allotments ranged from the $401.76 which went to Watauga County, to the $2,534.76 which went to Wake County. There were 86 counties.[24]

For the 53 school districts in Forsythe County, the range was from $6.50 to $176.34. The appropriation for the 79 Guilford County districts ranged from $23.04 to $186.24. The appropriation for each county was apportioned among the school districts by J. W. Alspaugh, Chairman of the Board of Superintendents.[25] On October 18, 1861, the Literary Fund of North Carolina ordered $90,452 distributed among the various counties in April, 1862. The Fund expressed the hope that the schools would be continued with the assurance that the expense would be met in April.[26]

The general school statistics for 1860-61 reported 3,484 school districts in the counties. Reports from 77 counties showed that there were 2,479 licensed teachers, 315 or 12.52 per cent of whom were women. There were 200,855 pupils, of whom 96,926 were boys, reported, but total attendance was only 105,048.

"It will be observed," Wiley said, "that there were nearly seven times as many male as female teachers," but the females "ought to constitute two-fifths of the whole number of teachers." There was, therefore, "honorable and useful employment in our State for at least seven hundred more of her virtuous and educated daughters."[27]

Since the school term averaged three and two-thirds months and the average salary was $26, the teacher might expect to earn less than $100 a year.

In the regular session of the 1860-61 Assembly, an act to provide funds for completion of the building to be occupied by the North Carolina Institution for the Deaf and Dumb and Blind "and other purposes" was ratified. It provided for the appropriation of only $2,000 to complete the building, $900 to teach book binding, and $100 for books.[28] The economic problems faced by the University of North Carolina were hardly less pressing, but the University could report encouraging progress. It announced on May 13, 1861, that it was indebted to the kindness of J. B. Neathery, publisher, for "a catalogue of this Institution for 1860-61." The University was then "one of the most popular and flourishing Institutions of the South," had a total enrollment of 376,[29] and had been in successful operation since February, 1775.[30]

Getting a legal education was less difficult than today, because there were no requirements as to time of study, no course prerequisites, and the nature of the course was more practical and less theoretical than now. Those who worked and studied law at the same time usually learned enough to pass the bar examinations within two years. Thomas L. Clingman, United States Senator from North Carolina when North Carolina seceded from the Union, applied to study law under direction of Thomas Ruffin, but Ruffin either refused to accept Clingman as a law student or failed to reply. Clingman, therefore, applied to, and was accepted by, William A. Graham.[31]

The lawyers had to "ride circuits," the fees were small, there was poor order in the courts and there was a lack of good lodging in the towns where the lawyers frequently had to pass the night. Yet the more courts attended, the more people they met, and the more they worked with their out-of-town clients the more quickly their reputation grew and spread. They carried their libraries in their saddles. Clients gave little and very indefinite information in a letter to their lawyer, making it necessary for him to try to see his client a few moments before court opened, yet there were no offices for consultation. Travel difficulty made most attorneys hesitate before accepting appellate work, and there were few appeals.

Nevertheless, Wiley had great faith at least in the common schools of the state, because in his eighth annual report to the General Assembly for 1860 he boasted that

The educational system of North Carolina is now attracting the favorable attention of the States South, West and North of us, . . . rapidly elevating the character of the State at home and abroad, and . . . worthy of the pride and fostering care of all classes of her patriotic citizens.

All modern statistical publications give us a rank far in advance of the position which we occupied in such works a few years ago. . . .

The State now has more of the elements of moral greatness than any of her sisters; and all desirable and endurable national prosperity must be based on moral power.

In a message to the Senate, Governor Ellis added: "under this system, the means of education in its primary branches are placed within the reach of every child in the State."

That Wiley and Ellis had impressed on the people the need for education in North Carolina is attested by the following letter from Jacob Garret to Judge Thomas Ruffin on December 3, 1861:

Mr. Thomas Ruffin
Dear Sir after my respects to you and thanks for favors past may I be permitted to address you as a friend and ask a favor at your hands on a subject that has lately bin [*sic*] impressed on my mind by seeing and knowing the disadvantagious [*sic*] my sons labor under for the waunt [*sic*] of of an education and the many appeals I see to parents to Educate ther [*sic*] children and an application made to President Davis to have a youth discharge [*sic*] from service in the Army whoo redily complyed [*sic*] and sayed [*sic*] that useing [*sic*] up Boys in the Army was like Grinding seed corn. I therefore wish to get my son from the army and send him to School if I can get a discharg [*sic*] for him, he has many good trates [*sic*] about him that will be lost to the community unless he can have a better Education. I therefore feel it my duty to make the effort to get him to school. now how to proseed is what I waunt [*sic*] to know is the subject of my writing to you if the Guviner [*sic*] is the proper one I waunt you to lay the matter before him and see if it can be done. I hope you will lend me your

influence to the matter he is in the 26th Regement [sic]
Col. Z. B. Vance Captain McLane when Sworn in but is
now Captain Lane Chatham Boys the name of the company
I therefore hope you will lend me your influence Please
write to me sooner as you assertain [sic] what can be done
direct your letter to Graham. Yours &c

JACOB GARRETT

the age of my son 18 his name is William Alex

GARRETT[32]

Closely connected with education in North Carolina were
ideology and propaganda. One of the leading agencies of
propaganda was the States Rights Party headed by Governor
Ellis.[33] That public opinion and propaganda are always
reflected in the press is indicated by the relations between
the *Standard,* which was also referred to as the *Daily Standard* and the *Daily North Carolina Standard,* and the *Weekly
State Journal,* both published in Raleigh. After Ellis addressed the Assembly on November 19, 1860, the *Standard*
reported that North Carolina bonds had been sold in New
York at the lowest rate at which these bonds had ever
been sold, and that as soon as Ellis' speech reached New
York an additional reduction might be expected. The
Weekly State Journal, which considered the *Standard* inconsistent, said the governor's speech was not threatening
to the North and that the *Standard* was welcome "to all it
can make of this mode of warfare." The governor's message
had reached New York, it reported, but North Carolina
stocks had gone up from 76 to 85, concrete proof that the
Standard was in error.[34]

In a message to the Assembly on November 20, 1860,
Ellis reported that the railroads could be depended upon to
pay reasonable dividends, because "they are constructed
mainly by slave labor, which . . . not requiring mechanical
skill, is undoubtly the cheapest that can be employed." He
said that

our great line of road from Beaufort to Cawana, (Duck Town) on the Tennessee line, a distance of five hundred sixty miles, will, when completed, cost $12,610,000. . . . On the other hand we find that the Erie road in New York, some four hundred miles in length, cost $32,000,000. . . . The cost of our road will be $22,500, while that of the Erie is $80,000 per mile. A clear profit on the former of $1550 per mile would give a dividend of 6 per cent, while on the latter it would require a nett [sic] profit of $4,800 per mile to give the same dividend.

This, he said, teaches that "there is a proper division of labor which, if observed, will avoid all possible conflicts of interests and endure to the advantage of all." This division, he said, consisted of the employment of slave labor where exercise of physical rather than mental capacity was required, and labor requiring skilled and educated reasoning faculties should be reserved for the white population, where he believed these facilities mainly and almost exclusively were to be found.

Under this system, Ellis said, the means of education in its primary branches were within the reach of every child.

At least $11,000,000 of the $12,000,000 of annual exports from North Carolina resulted directly from slave labor, he explained, and said it appeared to him that society was based on and sustained by slave labor, because there was scarcely an occupation or profession that did not mainly depend on it for support. Without this labor no railroads could be built, and those already constructed could not be maintained. The public credit rested on slave labor, because "the most productive part of our territory would not and could not be cultivated by the white race."[35]

A Raleigh newspaper reported on December 12, 1860, that the "submissionists" were endeavoring to class North Carolina with the border States. However, ten of the fifteen slave-holding States were nearer to free soil than North Carolina and further from the free States than any southern State, except South Carolina, Georgia, Florida, and Louisiana. It had fewer points on its seaboard from which slaves could escape to the North and fewer points at which an enemy could land on its coast than either of the States.[36]

Attempts were made to show that plenty of food was produced in the South but that this was not the case in the North. In 1850, the slave states produced 7,660,651 bushels of peas and beans, but the North produced only 518,833 bushels. Corn production in the South was 345,000,000 bushels, but only 223,000,000 bushels in the North. Southern sweet potato production was 37,136,812 bushels, but it was only 1,122,323 bushels in the North. While the South produced 215,312,210 pounds of rice, the North produced only 500 pounds. It was admitted that the value of the livestock production was $263,000,000 in the North and only $146,000,000 in the South, but it was quickly pointed out that there were "nearly twice the number of persons to support in the free States as in the slave States." Moreover, the South had the facility to produce, it was reported, and yearly produced as much provisions as the North.[37]

The condition of the slave, the free Negro, and the non-slaveholding white population was considered better than that of the North. The almost "4,000,000 of Negroes in the South" were "the most civilized and most christianized of any four millions of Negroes ever known to exist . . . ," this propaganda continued, but "if the supremacy of the white man over him were abolished, he would soon relapse into his original condition of savagery."[38] The non-slaveholder of the South was assured that the remuneration afforded by his labor, "over and above the expense of living," it was emphasized, was larger than wages in the free States. There were said to be fewer unemployed persons in the South. These unemployed were said to be migrating south, but no white worker had been forced to leave the South or to remain without employment. Yet that it would have been more accurate to say that "few white workers have been forced to leave the South or remain without employment" is shown by the following statement: "Such as have left emigrated from States where slavery was least productive." On the other hand, those who came to live almost anywhere in the South were "enabled soon to retire to their homes with a handsome competency." The statement was said to be "nearly as true for the agricultural as for other interests." Daily wages in New Orleans, Louisiana, Charleston, South Carolina, and Nashville, Tennessee were, for bricklayers, $2.50 to $3.50; carpenters, $2.25 to $2.75; and laborers, $1.00 to $1.50. Daily wages in Chicago, Illinois; Pittsburgh, Pennsylvania; and Toronto, Ontario (Canada), were: bricklayers, $1.00 to $2.00; carpenters, $1.50 to $1.75; and laborers, $.75 to $1.00. The weekly rate of board for laborers in the three southern States mentioned was compared with the rates in Illinois, Pennsylvania, and Massachusetts, and according to the 1850 census found to be as follows: Louisiana, $1.70; South Carolina, $1.75; Tennessee, $1.32; Illinois, $1.49; Pennsylvania, $1.72; and Massachusetts, $2.12. The annual wages of the agricultural classes as given in parliamentary reports, were as follows: France, $20.00 to $30.00, with board; and Italy, $12.00 to $20.00. After citing these selected statistics, it was concluded that in the United States, agricultural labor was highest in the Southwest and lowest in the Northwest—the South and North differing very little.[39]

"We must answer it" (the Civil War), one newspaper reported in June, 1861, "not as man to man but as *man* to *savage*." In such newspapers were headlines such as "Distress in the North, Strength in the South" or "Signs of Distress in New York." Quoting the New York Day Book, it was reported that in every direction there were homes and stores to rent and property for sale, at less than cost. These signs were hanging over some of the newest and most elegant structures. "From the Astor House to the corner of 14th

Street one could count 189 of these commercial epitaphs. If one were to slip quickly into many handsome establishments where plate glass vied with gilding as the adornment of happier days, it might be whispered to him that business was dead and the place soon to close."

That the South was greater than the North was attested by the fact that it contributed twice as many men in the Mexican War as the North did. With her fields cultivated and nearly all of the work done by slaves, "it could place almost her entire population under arms." In a great emergency, it was reported, the Southern States could place a million men in the field. On June 4, 1861, the *Belton* (Texas) *Independent* reported: "Wheat is being harvested this week, and will continue until finished. Never was there such a vast amount of grain in Texas. . . ." Oats and barley were expected to "make the largest yield we ever saw," and corn was to be made without additional rain. Two weeks later, however, a North Carolina newspaper suggested that

> The Governors of all the Southern States should at once issue their proclamation forbidding the distilling of grain into whiskey. All grain should be kept and used for food, and whiskey will be a curse to everybody. Let no more corn be used for distilling whiskey, at least until the war is over.

It was "most certainly true . . . the invaders in the North would subjugate and destroy" the South, "without mercy."[40] However, even the position of the Protestant Episcopal Church in the Confederate States of America seems to have been that slavery was justified. The official organ of the denomination reported in October, 1861, that

> . . . Negro slavery, in a temporal and political point of view, is a wise and beneficial institution—a benefit alike to the slave and master.[41]

As to the South's economic self-sufficiency, it should be noted that peas, beans, corn, sweet potatoes, and rice were not the only food items consumed, and far too few towns and occupations were included in the statistics on wages and cost of board. However, it was reasonable to expect that the South would contribute more men and fight more valiantly in the Mexican War than the North. The South felt that success in that war would lead to the extension rather than curtailment of slavery, ultimately strengthening the southern rather than the northern position in Congress by the admission of slave territory to the Union as slave states, or admission of territory into which the southern plantation owners might extend slavery. Thus, while the South might have done all that it could to win that war, the Northern States sought victory in defeat.

Chapter Five

The Church

THE church in North Carolina was as successful as it was in 1861 largely because it was supported by religion (albeit more appropriately written with a capital letter) and sanctioned by law. So strict was the observance of the Sabbath that even church conventions were generally scheduled for Friday, Saturday, and Monday—Sunday to be devoted largely to preaching. Work of a more laborious nature was forbidden and noise which would be tolerated on the other days of the week could lead to arrest.[1] Arrests had been made for card playing even during the week and when there was no betting.

It would be difficult, if not impossible, to ascertain precisely what denominations were prevalent in 1861. There are countless instances in which census information was either carelessly reported or carelessly recorded. The Arbor Church was reported as such in some instances, but also as the Arbor Reformed, Arbor Baptist, and the Arbor Methodist Church. The Catholic churches were reported as Catholic and as Roman Catholic. The Methodist Episcopal churches were sometimes reported as Episcopal Methodist, and the Methodist Protestant Churches were also reported as Protestant Methodist. Old Baptists, Old South Baptists, Old School Baptists, and New South Baptists were reported. Episcopal congregations were reported as Protestant Episcopal and Episcopal Protestant. The name of the church organization was sometimes changed to reflect the politics of the congregation, as indicated by the Primitive, Old South, and New South Baptists, the Methodist Episcopal Church, South, the Methodist Protestant Church, the Old South Presbyterian Church, the Southern Church, the Secessionist Church, the Southern Baptists, and the Presbyterian Church in the United States.

There were a few Evangelical Lutheran, German Reformed, Moravian, and Episcopal churches, and apparently only one each of the following churches: Protestant, Missionary Protestant, Evans Chapel Zion (reported as African Chapel), Southern, Union, Universalist, Low, Secession, and Publick [sic] church. The denomination of some of these churches could not be ascertained. Tyrell County reported one Free for All Church with a seating capacity of 250 and valued at $200. L. L. Foushee maintained a church in Carteret County with a seating capacity of 400, but whether he intended his own name to be the name or denomination of his church is not clear. In the poorer or more sparsely settled areas of the State extensive use was made of school buildings as places of worship. Surry County reported forty schools with an average seating capacity of 100 each, and valued at $50.00 each, in use as places of worship "for all denominations."[2]

Most of these congregations seem to have supported the South, but contemporary reports indicate that there was some disloyalty in the Beaufort area during the summer of 1861.

"It is rendered certain," the *Goldsboro Tribune* reported, "that a Methodist preacher of the name of . . . [sic] Taylor who was with the troops at Hatteras as a spiritual teacher," turned traitor. During the movement of troops from Fort Clark, "some say before the firing commenced, while other accounts . . . seem to indicate that . . . it was after the event," the Reverend Mr. Taylor lagged behind the troops until he was a mile and a half to the rear. Then he signaled the Union

troops who sent a boat and took him to the fleet. A souther-
ner married to a southern woman and with "a family of
children," surrounded "with the light of truth and having
all the social affections and patriotic emotions bearing upon
him," the *Tribune* concluded, "this man sinned against his
country."[3] At the same time it was reported that the Reverend Van Antwerpt, Episcopal preacher and teacher in Beaufort, had committed two grave acts of disloyalty. He had
"treated . . . with contempt the Fast Day recommended by
President Jefferson Davis by refusing to open his church on
that day, June 13, and failed to mention Thanksgiving Day
on the Sunday after the Manassas battle and victory. The
Tribune was gratified, however, because some of his members "ceased to attend his preaching."[4] Later that fall, the
Tribune requested the "Rev. Mr. Barrett" to report on
"affairs in Beaufort." His report contained the names of
"persons obnoxious to the severest censure." The *Tribune*
was unwilling to publish the names of individuals concerned,
but the reports started with the Episcopal Church. The
Baptists were reported "few in number," but even among
them were some who were disloyal to the South. There was
no organized body of Presbyterians, but Barrett gave a vivid
description of the vice of disloyalty in the Methodist Episcopal Church.

Many women and children were reported passing through
Goldsboro and others as establishing at least temporary residence there. Others evacuating the eastern combat zone had
taken other routes, as North Carolina prepared to resist.
The *Tribune* expressed the opinion that the Union troops
could not capture New Bern or if they did the people would
"set fire to every dwelling" rather than to permit it to fall
into the hands of the enemy.[5]

The Protestant Episcopal Church, however, reported the
slaves demoralized. The church owed the slaves instruction
and the Gospel with all of its moral and spiritual benefits,

an editorial in the official organ of the church contended; but when the condition of the slave was examined, it found that either the church was not performing its duty or the slaves were not profiting from the work of the church.

"Cases there may be found among them of sincere piety and real Christian rectitude," it was explained, "but little or nothing clearly illustrative of general moral and religious power for good. There is obviously a defect somewhere in these systems. The comfort of our condition" depended "to a very great extent upon the moral state of these people," and they were "so mixed up with us, so much . . . part and parcel of ourselves, that the sins of our servants come down upon our heads," the church reasoned; yet there was "very little ground for insurrection." This was true because "one good effect of the existing war . . . is the conviction the slave population are everywhere receiving of the vast and irrestible power of the whites."

The slaves were considered secure. If the South should win, they would be even more secure, but only for a while, because the slave population would increase and "endanger the security of Southern civilization."

While it was true that the South might keep the slaves in order by superior discipline and arms and force of numbers, the plea of the church was that the South should find a better way. This better way, it said, could be through "enactment of laws" which would "render their condition . . . equal to that of any laboring class in any country by kind treatment and . . . effective moral and religious training."[6]

The Presbyterian Church in the South also supported slavery. The Southern Presbyterians organized the Presbyterian Church in the United States which established a separate existence in 1861. At its General Assembly at Augusta, Georgia, that year, it adopted the following resolution:

First, that the standing committee appointed by the moderator "are, as usual, in the General Assembly of the

Presbyterian Church in the United States of America." Second, that the Assembly was to be governed by the rules of the church until otherwise ordered. Third, that the "style and title of this church shall be the Presbyterian Church in the Confederate States of America."[7] The Westminister Shorter Catechism was ratified by the General Assembly of the Presbyterian Church in the United States on December 4, 1861.[8] The Confederate Presbyterians expressed pleasure that hundreds of converts among the colored population were being added to the church,[9] and outlined its position on slavery.

Slavery, the church said, had been "a link in the wondrous chain of Providence through which many sons and daughters . . . have been made heirs of the heavenly inheritance." The providential results, however, were regarded as no justification "if the thing is intrinsically wrong," but slavery was considered "a matter of devout thanksgiving, and no obscure imitation of the will and purpose of God." This being true, perpetration of slavery was clearly the duty of the church.

The Assembly declared "the general operation of the system" to be "kindly and benevolent" and slavery to be a "real effective discipline." Without slavery, the church said it was "profoundly persuaded that the African race in the midst of us can never be elevated in the scale of being." As long as that race, "in its comparative degradation co-exists side by side with the white," the Assembly concluded, "bondage is its normal condition."[10] If the Presbyterians believed that slavery was the only means of elevating the African and that his degraded existence made bondage his "normal condition," perhaps they shared with the Episcopalians the professed belief that the slaves should be improved by "effective moral and religious training." Since neither church believed the slave had been sufficiently elevated to live among the white population, they joined in supporting the war.

First to attempt religious work in North Carolina were the Friends and the Church of England which were soon followed by the Baptists.

The Baptists

The 1860 religious census reported fifteen Baptist sects, but it was the Southern Baptists who withdrew from the General Missionary Convention in 1845 because of disagreement on the slavery question and formed the Southern Baptist Convention to which most Baptists adhered. The Free Will Baptists deserted the Southern Baptists because they could not agree on the question of slavery.

Because these sects were more prevalent, it was possible to gain some insight into the operations of the Baptist denomination. Most sects of this denomination apparently held their monthly business meeting on Saturday, although they were sometimes held on Sunday, and they were always preceded by a sermon if a minister was present.

In November, 1860, the Meherrin Baptist Church of Murfreesboro met after the sermon by Brother J. N. Hoggard. Prayer was followed by the roll call and the "door was opened for the reception of members."[11] The January, 1861, conference was postponed until February because of the funeral of Deacon Elisher Vaughan.[12] The Lufty Baptist Church in the Great Smokey Mountains National Park where in 1954 the building was still standing, held monthly meetings on Saturday before the fourth Sunday. Frequently no important business was transacted, the minutes consisting primarily of four words: "The church met, fellowship found." This scant statement was signed following the August, 1860, meeting by William Bradley, Moderator Pro Tem. Because of the extremely cold weather in November the church failed to meet. Church did meet for the Sunday services "and Brother Evins [sic] preached." The November

minutes were signed by R. Evins, Moderator. Church met in
January, 1861, and in February it met and chose Brother
Evins and Brother Henry Conner to serve as moderator and
moderator pro tem during the following year.[13] Minutes of
the Wheeler's Primitive Baptist Church in Yanceville indicate that a sermon was preached during the Sunday meeting when a minister was present. Always in the regular
sessions "fellowship was inquired for." This statement was
followed by the answer, "all in peace," or "all appear in
peace." At the May, 1861, meeting, the report was "not in
peace."[14]

The associations held their meetings in late summer or
fall. The One Hundred Third Session of the Sandy Creek
Baptist Association was held in the church at Mt. Vernon
Springs in Chatham County on October 4-7, 1861. Sunday
was devoted to preaching in the grove near the church.[15]
The Brown Creek Baptist Association held its seventh annual session in the church at Philadelphia in Union County
on October 11, 12, and 14. Sunday, October 13, was devoted
to worship. At 10:00 "a large crowd assembled under the
Arbor and spent one hour in prayer for our soldiers. . . ."
At twelve noon, Elder B. F. Whilden addressed the congregation at the Arbor on the subject of missions, after
which "a collection was taken up for missionary purposes
amounting to $12.65." Elder S. J. Fincher preached at the
same time "in the house." After a one-hour recess, those at
the Arbor were addressed on the subject of baptism by Elder
J. F. McLure according to appointment at the last meeting of
the Association. Elder A. L. Stough addressed those "in the
house."[16] Arrangement for Sunday worship had also been
made by the sixty-eighth annual session of the Yadkin
Baptist Association when it met in the Eaton's Church in
Davie County on October 5, 6, and 8, 1861. On Sunday,
October 7, Elder William G. Brown preached the ten
o'clock sermon in the church to "a large and well ordered

congregation." Elder R. H. Griffith preached the eleven o'clock sermon, after which "a collection" amounting to $16.91 "was taken up." Elder S. P. Smith preached the two o'clock sermon which closed the services for the day.[17]

Much of the time spent in these associations had to be devoted to business. For example, the fourteenth item on the agenda in the 1860 meeting of the Yadkin association was provision for printing the minutes. A. W. Martin, Association clerk, was appointed to prepare the minutes for the press and have eight hundred copies printed. The Association voted that he "be allowed $5 for his trouble."[18] The responsibility of managing the business affairs of the religious organization would bear even more heavily on the independent congregations in these associations. In 1860, the Meherrin Church reported that twenty-three members were added during October. The annual or deacon's meeting was held "on the first Lord's day in November" with William Vaughan as moderator. A resolution was passed which provided that Samuel Woodard "take care of the house" as he had formerly done "and receive for his services eight dollars" as for the previous year. The deacons resolved unanimously that Brother J. N. Hoggard "be requested to preach for us the ensuing year" and that he should receive the same salary " (which is $100) for his services." It was proposed in the December meeting of the church that a house be erected "for the entire use of candidates for baptism." William Vaughan and Lewis Parker were appointed "a committee" to take up subscriptions. If enough money were subscribed, they were also to act as members of the building committee.[19]

The July, 1861, minutes indicate that members were taken into and given letters of dismissal from Meherrin in church meetings after the sermon. Persons accused of offenses were mentioned and "a committee of two" appointed to cite them to appear in the church meeting on the Saturday of the next conference, "their report to be final." In the next meeting on August 3, two persons who had been thus cited appeared. They asked forgiveness, the church forgave them, and the charges against them were dismissed. Persons who desired assistance would write letters to the church meeting. In response to such a letter, the August meeting sent $3.60 to Thomas Bolton.

In the meeting on October 5, Deacon Elijah Vaughan preferred a charge against William Lawrence for profanity and immoral conduct. Upon what the church considered satisfactory proof, he was excluded from the church. No record could be found of his citing and appearance before the church meeting. In the regular meeting of the deacons in November the church again voted to pay Samuel Woodard eight dollars "to take care of the house as he has formerly done" for one year. Brother Hoggard was rehired at one hundred dollars.[20]

When the Three Forks Baptist Church at Boone met on the first Saturday in September, 1861, there was no business. The next day the church agreed unanimously to grant Brother Michael Cook, Jr., written license "to exercise his publick [sic] gift wherever the Lord may call him."[21]

The Primitive Baptist Church combined business and religion, because everything it did seemed to reflect the faith of the congregation. The Primitive Baptist, official newspaper of these communicants, was made up largely of letters to the newspaper itself. Addressed to "Brother Temple" these letters would contain two or three short sentences devoted to business. The writer would then take a text from the Bible and preach a sermon. "A few lines to the brethren and sisters scattered abroad in the different parts of the country" sometimes filled more than two full pages in the newspaper. These people expected to see not merely brief mention of the dollar they had sent to renew their subscriptions, but their entire discourse, sermon et al., published in the newspaper. The editor urged them to write. When their letters were delayed, they apologized and they were urged to write again.

On June 30, 1861, Robert Campen, writing from Washington, enclosed one dollar. He said he had sent one dollar for William Potter in April "to pay for 1861," for which he had a postmaster's receipt. He said he had not "seen it receipted" and would like to know "whether it came to hand or not." He then agreed to serve as agent for the newspaper.

John Vaughan, a slave at Rocky Mount, had a letter written to *The Primitive Baptist* on that same date. He enclosed one dollar to pay for his subscription to the newspaper which had expired. He apologized for being late in paying this bill, explaining that he had not been able to get anyone to write for him before that time. He expressed satisfaction that the newspaper had "thought enough of my pieces to publish them." Then he took a text from the Book of Genesis and concluded his letter.[22]

The moral advice, sermons, and testimonies contained in these letters served as a useful device for unifying the few scattered Baptists adhering to their doctrine.

The mission-minded Baptists expressed their missionary spirit in the fifty-fourth annual session of the Chowan Baptist Association held in Edenton on May 15 to 20, 1860. The Association defined colportage as "the work of our homes . . . the gospel taking possession of the printing press and bending it to the services of God—compelling the most powerful agency known to man to become a means of salvation." It said that "every lover of Christ loves colportage when he comes to know and understand it."[23]

The Yadkin Association said the duty of the Baptists in the State was to provide the people with means of salvation. The people were urged to do all they could for foreign and domestic missions, but, the Association explained, "the State missions have the first claim upon your beneficence."

It reported many areas in the State where there was no preaching by any denomination and urged the Baptists to assume the obligation of supplying, "as far as possible, the destitute with the preaching so much needed." All brethren with "any gift" were urged to use it for Christ in the destitute places adjacent to them, thus forming a nucleus of churches where there are now none." Sabbath schools were also urged in these areas, and as for colportage, the Association said it was "another good means . . . for supplying your destitution."

The Association had appointed twenty missionaries during the year. "The African mission," it was reported, "has lately assumed a very interesting phase. The colony of Liberia is regarded as being as promising as was the old Plymouth Colony." Other missions mentioned were Japan—where two missionaries had recently been appointed—China, and Brazil.[24]

The Liberty Baptist Association in its twenty-eighth annual session at Jersey Meeting House in Davidson County August 24, 25, and 27, 1860, also reported indifference toward missions. Temperance was reported neglected, and the youth was reported to be surrounded by and exposed to temptations. It was even feared that youth was being encouraged to make "moderate use of strong drink." The committee urged "united efforts in favor of temperance."[25]

In its report on missions in 1861, the Brown Creek Association asked:

> Shall the cause of God suffer? Shall the word perish, because christians love their money or themselves more than they love Christ? Let such remember who said, 'He that loveth houses and land or his own life more than me, is not worthy of me'. . . . Millions on millions have perished because professing christians have loved the things of this world more than the souls of men. The heathen now alive must receive the gospel or perish.[26]

Many of the Baptists placed great emphasis on education. The Chowan Association reported in May, 1860, that the Chowan Female Collegiate Institute was "still in a flourishing and prosperous condition." Wake Forest College had been in operation more than twenty years. "The condition of our colleges . . . is very encouraging," the Association reported, but warned that the Baptists would have to guard against "the education of beneficiaries of Pedo-Baptist denominations, free of tuition."[27] The Meherrin Church in its monthly church meeting in July of that year presented the pleas of the Sunday school and requested aid for the library. Thirty-one dollars was contributed.[28] The annual session of the Beulah Baptist Association at Hillsborough August 10 to 13 urged ministerial education. The whole State was reported calling for men to preach the Word. If God has called one to preach, the Association explained, "he ought to preach anyhow," but many were "kept back" in that age "by want of education." If children were called to preach, they were to be educated, and if licensed by their churches, the Association proposed to aid those who would need assistance in obtaining an education. The goal of the Association was "to have every young minister in the State to have the advantage of a course of study at our College."[29] The seventeenth annual session of the Union Baptist Association at Lebanon in New Hanover County on October 9 to 12 agreed that the whole state was "crying aloud for men to preach the word" and that many "called to preach" are kept back by lack of education. It not only urged that they be sent to Wake Forest College and that the parents do what they could to support them, but announced that "if they [are] pious and licensed by their churches," the Association would educate them. It also expressed the desire that every young minister in the State have the advantage of "a course of study at our College."[30]

At Raleigh, a "Baptist female school" was being established in 1860. The thirteenth annual session of the Tar River Baptist Association at Franklinton on August 23 to 25 passed the following resolution in support of the school at Raleigh:

> Resolved, That we have heard with much pleasure of the liberal efforts made by our brethren in Raleigh to establish at that point a first class Baptist Female School: that we regard such an enterprise at that place a denominational necessity and commend it to the favorable consideration of our brethren.[31]

The Sandy Creek Baptist Association meeting at the church at Gum Springs in Chatham County on October 2, was more realistic. Every community needs and must have a school, it agreed, but it was difficult, if not impossible, to sustain so many schools. Experience proves that many schools fail, the committee reported, and "it becomes our duty as wise men to ascertain the causes of these failures and prevent them." The policy recommended was to "have few schools, . . . rely on private enterprise for primary schools" and "establish more advanced schools on a solid money basis."[32]

The Pamlico Baptist Association in tenth annual session at Conconary in Halifax County on October 18 to 20, approved the following report on education:

> From whence originated the idea of civil liberty? Could it ever have been conceived in minds unlettered . . . ? To what are we, as a nation indebted for our rapid growth in attaining our present political position? . . . Minds aided by education. . . . An ignorant people may be duped, deceived, enslaved; but an intelligent one will be free. If we would retrograde—again become slaves—we have but to cease to foster a spirit of education.[33]

The third session of the Cedar Creek Baptist Association at Baptist Chapel Church in Sampson County on November 8 to 11, recommended that each Sabbath school have a

Sunday school library and question books for Bible classes. Each Sunday school was urged to take Sunday school papers, and each secular school was urged to "take a lesson in singing each day of school."[34]

Education of the ministers at Wake Forest was urged again in 1861. Parents were greatly concerned about the education of their children, the Brown Creek Association complained, but the Baptists seemed "indifferent about the education of our ministers." It reported other denominations as "seeing the great improvement of the age" and "sending out in every direction their ministers with enlarged views and liberal education." The world, then becoming refined and intelligent, would "go out to hear those men preach the word of God who possess the most commanding talents and the best cultivated minds. If we wish to sustain ourselves as a great denomination," the Association concluded, "we must thoroughly train the minds of our ministers and enable them to keep pace with the general and increasing intelligence of the age."

In this endeavor the Brown Creek Association recommended Wake Forest College where tuition "per session" was $25.00. Room rent was $1.00, a servant $2.50, and incidental expenses $2.00. "Good board" was available at $9.00 a month, "if paid strictly in advance," or $9.50, and laundry service was $1.00 a month.[35] The most extreme notion regarding ministerial education was expressed in the report on that subject by the Cape Fear Baptist Association meeting at Antioch in Robeson County late in October. Education was to supersede the necessity of a change of heart or a divine call, the Association reported, because the Lord had committed the preaching of the Gospel to human instrumentality. Consequently, "we may naturally expect more will be accomplished by a man of cultivated mind . . . than by one whose qualifications are of an inferior grade."[36]

These associations, like the Protestant Episcopal and Presbyterian churches, also supported and were greatly affected by the war. The Liberty Association adopted a motion on Saturday, August 23, that a collection be taken up on the following Sunday to purchase Testaments for the soldiers. It amounted to $29.73 and was "paid over to the Treasurer for this purpose. J. B. Jackson, Moderator of the Association, William Owen, Wiliam H. Hammer, and A. Williams constituted "a committee to purchase Testaments for the soldiers," to report their proceedings at the next annual meeting of the Association. A. Williams was appointed to act as treasurer for the committee.[37]

The church at Mill River met after services on August 24, and gave serious consideration to the condition of the country. The committee appointed "to arrange and build an addition to our meeting house" reported that "on account of the troublesome times we think it not expedient to undertake the building at the present."[38]

The second annual session of the United Baptist Association, at Concord Church in Alexander County on October 18 to 20, approved extensive resolutions concerning the war. The Association described the war as "brought on by the unprovoked jealousies, angers, and despotism of a sectional party in the North, . . . bent on our subjugation and destruction." It invoked the presence and assistance "of the king of nations" in behalf of the South, and prayed "that this most unhappy and uncalled for struggle . . . be brought to a speedy and honorable close." United Association was not composed of "devotees of war," it was explained, but it was "a source of gratification to know that the Baptists of our country have taken a noble stand in defense of our rights and liberties." It had learned that "our brethren, Elders J. G. Bryan, R. L. Steele, and James Reed, had succeeded in raising a volunteer company, composed mostly of Baptists and commanded by the above-mentioned brethren. It, therefore, took "great pleasure in recommending them to the favorable consideration of the Baptist denomination, wherever their lot may be cast during the service."

The Association then resolved to set aside Thursday, November 7, as a day of public fasting and prayer "for the building up of Zion, the peace and prosperity of our country, and a speedily deliverance from our present condition."[39]

Most of these associations were composed of churches with colored members, and in many of the congregations the colored membership was larger than the white membership.

In 1860, the Pamlico Association contained ten congregations with colored members varying from one to eighty-seven in the Association. Churches with the largest number of colored members were Conconary, where the annual meeting was held, with eighty-seven; Greenville, twenty-eight; Goldsboro, twenty-one; Union, twenty-four; and Hancocks, eighteen.[40] The Pee Dee Baptist Association convened in its forty-fifth anniversary session at the forks of Little River in Montgomery County October 20 to 22. It contained two congregations with colored members, Spring Hill with 50 white and 81 colored, and Pleasant Grove with 57 white and 64 colored members.[41] The Liberty Association contained 14 congregations, three of which had colored members.[42] Beulah Association contained 56 congregations, four of which contained colored members. The churches with colored membership in the latter association were Beulah, with 105 colored and 59 white, Bear Marsh with 140 colored and 50 white, Johnson's Mission House with 166 colored and 130 white members; and Washington Church with 55 colored and 29 white members.[43]

In 1861, the Conconary Church in the Pamlico Association reported 97 colored members.[44] The Tar River Association met in 1861 at the Maple Spring Church in Franklin County on August 22 to 24. There were 24 churches in the Association and five, Bear Breek, Brown's, Louisburg, Perry's Chapel and Reedy Creek, with colored members.[45]

The Christian Church

The 1860 census lists two Christian sects, the Disciples, referred to alternately as Disciples or Christians, and the Baptist Christians. Some Baptists were reported as Christian Baptists. There was, therefore, a close connection between the Baptists and the Christians in North Carolina. The Disciples of Christ or International Union of Christians, an American movement for Christian unity, was founded by Thomas Campbell and his son, Alexander, in 1809. This church did not seem to develop rapidly in North Carolina, because there was apparently a conflict in the ideology upon which its organizational structure was based. Like the Baptist Church, it was congregational and democratic in government, but at the same time it fostered universalism. The dissident groups who left England and settled in the colonies south of Quebec did so partly because after the Reformation they could agree on religious principles with neither the Roman Catholic Church nor the Church of England. Thus, the violent dislike for the Church of England which was associated with oppression in the colonies was moderated but none the less transferred to the Protestant Episcopal Church in the United States after the American Revolution. Both Episcopalian and Catholic were less popular in North Carolina at the beginning of the Civil War.

The Universalist National Convention in 1860 in its report on the denomination, referred to the relation of the child to the church, and concluded:

> The Romanish and Episcopal Churches have the right theory on this subject. Children are born into the church by nature of their birth from Christian parents, and should be treated as belonging to it.

The Carolina Christian Monthly clipped these lines from the Religious Herald, Richmond, Virginia, and added its own comments. It appeared to *The Carolina Monthly* that universalism was becoming orthodox, so it declared:

> . . . Their National Convention have adopted the Romanish and Episcopal *dogma* that children born of Christian parents are born into the church and should be treated as belonging to it. . . . Fortunately, however, for the dominant race, the African is now slow to believe in Universalism. To their credit be it recorded.[46]

The Christian Church in 1861 was small in number but it was playing a leading role in the religious and educational life of the State.

The Methodists

When the General Conference of the Methodist Episcopal Church opened on Tuesday morning, May 1, 1860, in Buffalo, New York, a committee of forty-seven on slavery and a committee of seven on colored membership were appointed. The North Carolina delegates were Cyrus Nutt, John B. Birt, Jacob Colcazer, and Lonson W. Monson, and the reserves or alternates were Augustus Eddy and John Bradshaw.[47] Not a single member was reported in the Methodist Episcopal Church in North Carolina, but more than 44,000 members were reported that fall by the Methodist Episcopal Church, South, or 31,806 white members and probationers and 13, 182 colored members and probationers.[48] However, the Annual Conference of the Methodist Episcopal Church, South, in session at Nashville, Tennessee, reported 40,865 members and probationers—28,822 white and 12,043 colored. It is not possible to determine the precise number of members in the Methodist Episcopal Church, South, in North Carolina in 1860, because the members in the western part of the state were in the Holstein Conference and Wytheville, Abingdon, Rogerville, Knoxville, Cumberland, Chattanooga, Athens, and Asheville constituted that conference.[49]

The North Carolina Conference, held at Salisbury December 5 to 11, reported "a Raleigh City Mission" with 75 members and probationers, ten of whom were colored. A Raleigh colored mission had 264 "full members" and 72 probationers. One parish had 200 white members and there was a Raleigh circuit with colored and white members and probationers.[50] Churches in three districts in the Conference either had all colored members and probationers or colored members exceeded the total number of white members and probationers, and were distributed as follows:

The Washington District: 218 white and 494 colored.

The Fayetteville District; Fayetteville—Evans' Church Mission, 347 colored; Fayetteville Circuit, 338 white and 405 colored; Pittsboro, 47 white and 113 colored; and Robeson, 650 white and 652 colored.

The Wilmington District: Wilmington—Front Street, 255 white and 990 colored and Fifth Street, 182 white and 243 colored; Topsail, 165 white and 186 colored; Duplin, 391 white and 581 colored; South River Mission, 24 white and 168 colored; Elizabethtown, 385 white and 672 colored; Whiteville, 254 white and 327 colored; Cape Fear Mission, 350 colored; and North East, 93 white and 148 colored.[51]

The 1861 conference was held in Louisburg on December 4 to 9. The members in Hatteras, Ocracoke, and Portsmouth were not reported, but there was a total of 28,412 white and 12,593 colored members and probationers, indicating a slight decline in the white membership and a slight increase in the total membership and the colored membership during the preceding year.[52]

The *Methodist Almanac, 1860,* reported 31,435 white and 13,195 colored members and probationers in 1860, and 31,507 white and 13,145 colored members and probationers in 1861. These figures indicate a very slight increase in the total white and a very slight decline in the total colored members and probationers.[53] It is to be noted, however, that the *Almanac* reports were taken from old statistics, and because of the dues and obligations imposed in the Methodist conferences, the State conferences were likely to report smaller memberships. There was a decline in the colored membership in the Holston Conference in 1861.[54]

In 1861, there were in the Raleigh District, Raleigh City with 205 white members, Raleigh City Mission with white and colored members, Raleigh Colored Mission with 278 members and 31 probationers, and the Raleigh Circuit with white and colored members.

Districts with congregations consisting of all colored or more colored than white members were as follows:

Washington District: Washington, 208 white and 473 colored; and Bath, 185 white and 194 colored.

Newbern [*sic*] District: Newbern—Andrew Chapel Mission, 731 colored; and Bath—Purvis Chapel Mission, 240 colored.

Fayetteville District: Fayetteville—Evans' Church Mission, 311 colored; and Fayetteville Circuit, 358 white and 430 colored.

Wilmington District: Wilmington—Front Street, 245 white and 1,000 colored and Fifth Street, 159 white and 215 colored; Topsail, 165 white and 186 colored; Duplin, 186 white and 328 colored; South River Mission, 32 white and 194 colored; Elizabethtown, 361 white and 400 colored; Whiteville, 254 white and 327 colored; Magnola, 218 white and 231 colored; Cape Fear Mission, 350 colored; and North East, 97 white and 170 colored.[55]

These members were supporting four colleges, one high school, one female academy, and one female seminary, inherited from the Methodist Episcopal Church, in 1860. In the twenty-fourth session of the North Carolina Conference of the Methodist Episcopal Church, South, held at Salisbury December 5 to 11, in the Trinity College report it was explained that the College was "doing good work, the scholarship . . . sound and thorough, the discipline enobling and good—and the whole tone of life such as would exert a good moral influence. . . ." The boarding facilities were reported good and "at least two hundred young men could be accomodated."

Raised during the past year was $8,926 in cash and bonds payable in one, two, three, and four years after date—the largest amount ever reported by any agent appointed by the Conference to any agency of the church. The Conference resolved that the College deserved the confidence and support of the church and that the ministers distribute the college catalogue and represent the College. The Rev. N. H. D. Wilson was reappointed to continue the agency.

An announcement in the *Minutes* listed the Trinity faculty as the Rev. B. Craven, President and Professor of Mathematics, Rhetoric, and Logic; L. Johnson, Professor of Mathematics; W. T. Ganaway, Professor of Ancient Languages and History; J. L. Wright, Professor of Natural Science; O. B. Carr, Tutor of Ancient Languages and English Literature; and L. W. Andrews, Tutor of Mathematics. Tuition was "fifty dollars per annum," board was $7.00 to $7.50 per month, and board, including "washing, room, fuel, servants, etc.," $9.00 to $10.00 per month. It was located five miles from High Point on the Central Railroad.

Greensboro Female College at Greensboro was also a Methodist school. It reported one hundred sixty students in regular attendance on the campus and twenty-seven in private homes near the College. The Reverend T. M. Jones was the president. Other Methodist schools were Warrenton Female College, Wayne Female College, Olin High School for Male and Female pupils, Jonesville Male and Female Academy, and Glenn Anna Female Seminary at Thomasville. The Conference expressed confidence in and praised them all.[56]

The Methodist Protestant Church

The Methodist Protestant Church was originally composed of members from the Methodist Episcopal Church who separated over complaints that arose in the Conference of 1820. This complaining sect demanded that the local ministry be given the same rights, privileges, and representative voice in rule-making as the itinerancy. Reform groups called Union Societies were organized in Baltimore, North Carolina, Ohio, and New York. The loyalists in the church were referred to as "our old side brethren." A committee of the Society was authorized to devise a plan of separation, if their attempt to achieve reconciliation failed, and report it to the church. They lost the lower decision and the appeal to the Annual Conference and, destitute of a place of worship, were accomodated by the Presbyterian and Episcopal Churches. They finally organized a church in 1830, retaining the same doctrine, *sans* bishops, presiding elders, and other life officials. This left laymen and ministers equal in power and number in representation.

This spirit of equality was prevalent in the thirty-fifth session of the North Carolina Conference of the Methodist Protestant Church at Yadkin Institute in 1860. Meeting from November 14 to 20, the Conference resolved that "whenever any brother's name is called for examination, he shall retire from the house." However, they did not always follow this rule. The name of Q. Holton was called but the examination of his character was waived due to his absence. When the name of R. R. Michaux was called, his character examination was accomplished by direct questioning and on motion "his character passed." The name of Alston Gray was called "and questions propounded in his absence." Then "he was called in and an examination pursued in his presence by means of questions." When the name of G. A. T. Whitaker was called the examination of his character was waived on account of the absence of the delegate from Roanoke Circuit.

The church had nineteen circuits or missions, the number of churches in each circuit varying from none for Hamilton Mission to twelve in Guilford Circuit and Randolph Circuit. There were a total of 5,682 white members and 297 colored members. The total value of the church property was $47,460.

Because of its success during the past year, it was recommended that Monroe Mission "be erected into a circuit." A church had been erected and received by the quarterly conference of the Halifax Circuit. It was outside the jurisdiction of the circuit and could not legally belong to it without an extension of its boundaries. The Conference recommended that it either extend the boundary of the Halifax Circuit to include the new church or "transfer the said house of worship to Tar River Circuit." The circuits and missions reported a total of six hundred dollars.[57]

The Conference had convened at noon on November 14. By Friday morning, the week long conference had completed much of the important business of the church and turned to education. The principal educational obligation of the Conference was Yadkin Institute. A resolution was introduced providing, first, that the Institute be incorporated as a college; second, that the Conference appoint a committee of three to prepare a bill for the said incorporation; and third, that the Conference appoint a general agent to take up subscriptions for the use of said college, "with power to appoint one or more sub-agents for said purpose." The first two items were adopted. All three of them were adopted as amended on Saturday morning.

A committee composed of Alson Gray, David Weesner, D. L. Michael, John A. Davis, and Alexander Robbins reported that the Institute had a total indebtness of nine hundred dollars.[58]

Membership statistics for the Methodist Protestant Church in 1861 could not be found. On the basis of statistics reported by the Conference of the Methodist Episcopal Church,

South, and total membership figures reported by the Methodist Protestant Church for 1860, and considering the membership of the Methodist Episcopal Church, South, in the Holston Conference and the Portsmouth Conference, there were an estimated 60,000 Methodists in North Carolina in 1861.

The Society of Friends

The nineteenth-century Friends were divided into various groups. The Orthodox Friends and the Hicksite division resulted during 1827 and 1828 due to a dispute over the theological teachings of Elias Hicks. In 1845, about 500 Friends separated from the parent group in New England and became known as the Willwrite Separation. There were minor changes in the Hicksite and Orthodox Friends which led to several groups of congregational Friends, an anti-slavery group in Indiana, the Primitive Friends, and a special meeting of Friends in Philadelphia. They all maintained local or preparative monthly, quarterly, and yearly meetings.

Some of the younger Friends were expelled from the meetings during the American Revolution. Some left the main body of the society voluntarily. In Philadelphia an independent society called the Free Quakers was organized.

The Friends were extremely religious and greatly concerned about the temperance problem and strict observance of Sunday. In the 1860 yearly meeting at New Garden from November 5 to 9, the members of the North Carolina society were divided into "quarters," each of which made a "report on spiritus liquors." These reports showed a total of 1,361 members who did not use these liquors, eighty-one who admitted drinking liquor, and seventy-one who had not been questioned.[59] A similar report in 1861 indicated little if any change or improvement.[60] As for the observance of Sunday, the meeting offered the following advice:

Let us . . . abstain from all visiting and traveling and all business of a secular kind . . . not required by necessity or in acts of mercy or charity on that day, also from gathering into companies for social intercourse or light amusements, hunting, fishing, pleasure riding, and such like. And let us meet together for the worship of almighty God, and be careful to make a profitable and religious use of those portions of time of the First-day of the week which are not occupied by our meetings for worship.[61]

The 1861 meeting, beginning on November 2 also at New Garden, expressed grave concern about the poor attendance of the Friends meetings, particularly those held in the middle of the week, and issued the following warning:

It is doubtless true that worship may be performed alone, at our own houses or even in our fields, but we are *social* beings. Love of God begets love of man and this love of man is spoken of in the Scriptures as the proof that we are Christ's disciples. . . .

It is the settled conviction of experienced minds that there is among us too much of a running after the vain and frivilous fashions of the world, and that if we ever gain the position we are intended to occupy as a Religious Society, or even maintain our present standing, we must be purged from many things now among us.[62]

Because of extreme persecution there was a decline in the Friends membership. As a result the 1860 yearly meeting reported a deficit of $14,997.41 as of November 9. A proposed sum of $500.00 "to augment the yearly meeting stocks" was apportioned among the quarters as follows: First, $102.00; Western, $102.00; Deep River, $102.00; Southern, $102.00; Contentena, $47.00; New Garden, $25.00; and Lost Creek, $20.00.

The Trustees of the New Garden Boarding School made their sixth annual report. They reported 63 students, 30 members and 33 non-members, enrolled during the first session and 76 students or 39 members and 37 non-members, enrolled during the second term. There were six day students each term. The school had accounts payable amounting to $2,893.83 and its indebtedness was $2,937.00. Provisions on hand were valued at $744.58. It had gained $399.38 through various transactions during the year, spent $194.12 for repairs and had a balance of $205.26.

In the 1861 meeting, John Carter, treasurer of the Common Fund, reported $1,998.41 in cash and $530.00 in notes, $235.00 of which were believed worthless, "and $295.00 of which something possibly may be had." The interest had not been paid but was "ready to be paid." Allen U. Tomlinson, treasurer of the Charity Fund, had $1,005.93 at interest. He had collected and paid to the superintendent of the Boarding School $112.70, the total interest and some past due interest on the Fund. His report was signed for the committee by P. B. Benbow.

The Boarding School indebtedness was apportioned among the Quarters as follows: Western, sometimes reported as First Quarter, $40.80; Western, $34.80; New Garden, $10.00; Contentena, $20.40; Lost Creek, $12.00; Deep River, $41.20; and Southern, $40.80. The quarters were directed to raise the money as apportioned and pay it to Isham Cox, agent, to be applied to the liquidation of the debt. Lost Creek was not represented at the 1861 meeting.

In their twenty-fifth annual report, the Trustees of New Garden School reported debits and credits amounting to $257.03. The first session enrollment was 54, or 30 members and 24 non-members, and there was one day student. There were 23 members and 19 non-members enrolled in the second session and there were four day students.[63]

The only significant antislavery movement in colonial times occurred among the Friends. Although William Penn owned slaves and slavery was deeply interwoven into the fabric of American Quaker life, George Fox explained the basic inconsistency between slaveholding and Christianity.

He perceived of the spiritual danger inherent in this re-
lationship in 1657, and in 1671 suggested that African slaves,
like white slaves, should eventually be freed. His first sug-
gestion was that this should be accomplished after thirty
years.

By the eighteenth century, antislavery sentiment began
to show itself on both sides of the Atlantic and by 1775 the
Friends generally had condemned the members of the Society
who refused to abandon this practice. Virginia Friends dis-
couraged the buying and selling of slaves in 1768. North
Carolina Friends prohibited the purchase of any more slaves,
except for reasons approved by the monthly meetings, such
as preventing the breaking up of slave families in 1772.
Maryland Friends prohibited the purchase of slaves in 1762.
In 1768, they directed the monthly meeting to "disown such
persons as disorderly walkers until they so far come to a
sight or sense of their misconduct as to condemn the same
to the satisfaction of the said monthly meeting."

It was difficult for the Friends whose plantations depended
on slave labor to cease buying slaves, but neither the American Friends who most vigorously opposed ending this trade,
nor the brethren farther south, wished to oppose the majority of English and American Friends. Since they could not
purchase new slaves as needed and sell rebellious or super-
annuated ones, they could not continue as slaveholders, and
within a few years the Friends had given up slavery entirely.

These Friends not only sustained heavy losses, but in
North Carolina their antislavery policy led to persecution.
In December, 1861, the North Carolina Convention attempted to pass "an ordinance concerning Test Oaths and
Sedition." It would have required every free male person
in the State above sixteen to appear publicly and renounce
all allegiance to the Government of the United States and
promise "to support, maintain, and defend the independent
Government of the Confederate States." The alternative

would be banishment within thirty days. It was protested and failed.

Although every means was employed to prevent it and many were arrested and returned, many Friends left the State during the war. Some were included in the draft, but obtained their release on various grounds. There were three thousand Friends in 1851, but only two thousand in 1861. This decrease "was entirely due to emigration" and emigration continued throughout the war.[64] New Garden was thus threatened with termination throughout the war.

The Roman Catholic Church

The Catholic population was a much smaller and less controversial force than the Friends. North Carolina in 1860 was in the Charleston Diocese which was organized in 1820 and included the Bahama Islands. The Right Reverend Patrick N. Lynch was the bishop.[65] The Religious Census reported ten churches in North Carolina, distributed as follows:

County	Number	Total Value
Beaufort	1	$1,000.00
Northampton	1	15,000.00
Wake	1	7,500.00
Chowan	1	8,000.00
Cumberland	1	9,000.00
Alamance	3	4,200.00
Craven	1	800.00
Montgomery	1	4,000.00[66]

The precise number of parishes could not be ascertained, but communicants were being served at Charlotte, Concord, Coalmines in Chatham County, Edenton, Fayetteville, Greenfield, Greenwood, Halifax, Scotland Neck, New Bern, Plymouth, Raleigh, in Gaston County, Smithville, Washington, and Wilmington. The Rev. Thomas Quigley, pastor of St. John the Baptist Church at Raleigh, attended St. Patrick's Church at Fayetteville and Coalmines. The Rev. C. J. Croghan, pastor of St. John the Evangelist Church in Washington, attended New Bern, Edenton, and Plymouth. The Rev. Thomas Murphy, pastor of St. Thomas Church in Wilmington, served Smithville, Greenfield, Greenwood, Halifax, and Scotland Neck. There was a parish in Charlotte, St. Peter's, and two in Gaston County, St. Joseph's and St. Mary's. The Rev. Augustus F. McNeall, the pastor of the three parishes, also served Concord.[67] Thus, there seem to have been only seven parishes with churches, St. Peter's at Charlotte, St. Patrick's at Fayetteville, St. John the Baptist at Raleigh, St. Joseph's and St. Mary's in Gaston County, St. John the Evangelist at Washington, and St. Thomas at Wilmington. Catholics were being served in 16 communities. There were 10,000 Catholics in the Diocese of Charleston.

This general plan was in effect in 1861, except that the Reverend Mr. Croghan had acquired a new church, St. Paul's at New Bern.[68]

The first Raleigh church was opened on lower South Wilmington Street in 1839, with the Reverend Peter Whelan as the pastor. Subsequent changes in the growth and development of the city rendered the small frame structure "on a retired street" unsatisfactory. In 1859, the Baptist church on the southeast corner of Capitol Square (at the intersection of Wilmington and Morgan Streets) was offered for sale. It was acquired, "fitted up tastefully" as a Catholic Church, and dedicated during a visit by Archbishop John Hughes on Sunday, June 3, 1860.

Bishop N. Lynch arrived in Raleigh on Friday morning and Archbishop Hughes, on the way to the University of North Carolina where the students had invited him three times to deliver the commencement address, arrived that afternoon. Both "stopped at the Yarborough House" and on

Saturday "several distinguished citizens of Raleigh called on the Archbishop."

Attended by the Reverend Thomas Quigley, pastor of the church, the Reverend Thomas Murphy, pastor of St. Thomas at Wilmington, the Reverend C. J. Croghan, pastor of St. John the Evangelist at Washington, and the Reverend Mr. McNeirny, Bishop Lynch solemnly dedicated the church on Saturday morning and preached twice. Archbishop Hughes preached that afternoon.

Advance notice was given in the local newspapers and the church was filled "to the utmost capacity by perhaps the most respectable audience ever assembled in a Catholic church in Raleigh." Most of this audience was non-Catholic and included many anti-Catholics. The first mass was offered in the church in March, 1861.[69]

The events that disturbed the conditions in North Carolina described up to this point are the subject of the second part of this book.

PART II

North Carolina Drifts toward Secession

PART I of this book contains a brief survey of the social history of North Carolina. The problem now is to determine why North Carolina seceded from the Union. There is no simple answer, but the writer's theory is that although States' rights secessionists seem to have been a majority from the beginning, there was in fact a small group of States' rights secessionists, a small pro-Union group, and the majority of the population led by secessionists or pro-Unionists, depending on which group was the more dynamic and produced the better propaganda.

In the early days, the North Carolina colony was a refuge for men of small means who sought to improve their fortunes. In 1861, the small planter was still the chief factor in individual life. There was a serious lack of unity among the people due to diversity of ethnic origins and sectional influences. The balance of power was held by the section east of Raleigh until 1835, but long after reforms were made, this feeling continued as a potent force in politics. Except in a group of middle eastern counties, the slave system was never extensively developed. The vast number of non-slave-holding whites thus had great influence.

On every public question, there seemed to be a variety of public opinion and such conservatism as existed in North Carolina was perhaps nothing more than the failure of the people to unite in one common opinion and on one common program. There was prejudice against various political questions which tended to divide the State. There had been controversy over distribution of the federal lands after 1850, the States' rights group favoring the States and the Whigs favoring the central government. Taxes were higher on land than on slaves, thus encouraging purchase of slaves instead of land. The mechanic had to pay ten dollars per thousand on his tools, while the slaveholder paid only fifty cents a thousand on his slaves.

The non-slaveholding class upheld the States' rights secessionists who sought to protect their slave property because they were educated in the same ideology as the slaveholder and were connected with them by kinship and economic ties. The pro-Unionist and neutral population was not interested in a convention because they were satisfied within the Union. The secessionists struggled to secure authority for a convention, to consider the question of secession. However, there were several risks involved in calling a convention. The secessionists who advocated a convention said it was to preserve the Union; but when they met in convention they seceded and declared North Carolina an independent state. They advised the people that calling a convention would do no harm, because the question of secession would be submitted to the people, yet not one of the first five States that seceded, although acting under no emergency, submitted its action to the people. Besides, North Carolina did not have sufficient time to exhaust its constitutional remedies before the convention assembled. When enabling legislation was ratified, since they were far more interested in the convention than the pro-Unionists and neutrals, most of the delegates selected were secessionists. Thus, a vote for a convention became synonymous to a vote for secession. Moreover, North Carolina was isolated from the Union when Virginia seceded on April 17, and the second blockade on April 27 applied to North Carolina as well as Virginia.

The principal reason why North Carolina seceded was, therefore, the successful domination of the various conflicting groups in the State by the secessionists which led to the calling of the convention which they also dominated. Secession of Virginia thirteen days before the North Carolina convention and the blockade of North Carolina as well as Virginia three days before the North Carolina convention, helped to crystallize opinion in favor of secession.

However, the stage for secession had already been set in North Carolina prior to this event.

Chapter Six

The Eve of Secession

NORTH CAROLINA, like Virginia and Maryland, was a principal producer of tobacco. A State in which little cotton was grown, it remained an enclave of antique republicanism with fewer slaves than its neighbors. There were free Negroes in each of the eighty-seven counties, except Haywood where there were only 313 slaves. The leading slaveholding counties were Granville with 11,086, Wake with 10,733, Warren with 10,401, Halifax with 10,349, and Edgecombe with 10,108 slaves. There were far more slaves than white population in Edgecombe, Halifax, and Warren Counties, but slightly more white persons, 11,-189, in Granville County than slaves. The total State population was as follows: white population, 631,489; slave population, 331,081; and free Negro population, 30,097.

What North Carolina and the other States in the upper South wanted was peace, conciliation, and respect for Southern rights *within* the Union. Thus there was resentment both against secession agitation and the trouble-making abolitionists. The non-slaveholders were perhaps more ardent in their support of slavery than the planters, because they had in their minds a fixed and definite meaning attached to the word "abolitionist." They regarded it as meaning one who was in favor of setting all Negroes free to remain among the white population and have the rights and privileges of, and be on a basis of equality with, the poor white man. Having voted against secession, however, North Carolina was in the incredible or paradoxical position of a Union enclave until May 20 when it ratified the Confederate constitution. It is to be noted that the struggle against secession and for peace in North Carolina did not cease after the State had seceded from the Union. The Reverend James McNeill of Ashboro discontinued his subscription in a letter dated March 16, 1861, to the *Presbyterian* because it advocated secession and was "seeking to alienate one section of this country against the other." On December 9, 1861, it was reported that "Stewart, the great New York Dry-goods man," had contributed five hundred dollars to the "Relief Fund of loyal citizens of North Carolina." Stewart's letter was as follows:

> Dear Sir: It gives me great pleasure to send you a check for $500 for the Relief Fund for loyal citizens of North Carolina for which State I have ever had a warm affection, and I cherish the hope that she will be among the first to be restored to that Union of which she was so true a friend and from which she has been nominally severed against the real interest and wishes of her substantial people.[1]

More than one hundred peace meetings were held within two months in North Carolina after the Battle of Gettysburg on August 3, 1863, in order to promote negotiations for reunion. We might contend that Abraham Lincoln's call for militia in North Carolina led Governor John W. Ellis to send a prompt and indignant rejection and to call the Assembly into extra session for the purpose of summoning a convention. It could be contended that the call for troops in one flash served to alienate the whole mass of pro-Union sentiment which, while not pro-Lincoln, was not secessionist and constituted Lincoln's best chance of saving the Union without war. However, the convention ultimately was solely responsible for the secession decision.

The North Carolina delegation in Charleston in 1860 favored cooperation with the Union. Jonathan Worth opposed arming the state, combatted secession, and resisted the calling of a convention to consider secession. He abhorred both the northern abolitionist and the southern secessionist whom he said were actually cooperating to break up the Union. Perhaps the best proof that the convention delegates were secessionist and responsible for secession is that Worth steadfastly refused to become a delegate to the convention, the convention voted to secede on the first day of its first session, and there was not a single dissenting vote.

Senator Thomas L. Clingman of North Carolina, a member of the Thirty-sixth Congress, said on March 8 that it was understood that the State of Texas had "seceded from the Union" and was "no longer one of the United States." Then he introduced a resolution that Texas was not entitled to any representation in the Congress.[2] On the following Monday, Senator L. T. Wigfall of Texas said he believed that Texas had seceded, but unless he should receive official evidence of secession or unless the Senate should object, he would remain in the Senate. Clingman accused the Texas senator of pursuing the same policy of the senators from the other seceding States, remaining in Washington "from day to day, avowing that their purpose was to wait for official information."[3] Texas having seceded on February 1, Senator Clingman recommended on March 14 that the President "by and with the advice of the Senate, make a treaty with those States" (South Carolina, Georgia, Alabama, Florida, Mississippi, Louisiana, and Texas) that had seceded from the Union.[4] A resolution that Albert G. Brown and Jefferson Davis of Mississippi, Stephen R. Mallory of Florida, Clement C. Clay of Alabama, Robert Tooms of Georgia, and Judah P. Benjamin of Louisiana be expelled was introduced in the Senate on May 13. The motion to suspend Senator Wigfall, however, was before the Senate until mid-May, having been referred to the Judiciary Committee on May 12.[5]

On November 20, 1860, H. C. Douglas expressed regret "that the Democrats lost and Lincoln was elected," but asked:

. . . But Mr. Lincoln has been constitutionally elected to the presidency, and however much we may regret the success of a sectional party, is it not the duty of all good citizens to submit to the popular will, unless an overt act be committed by the party? . . .

Writing from somewhere in Maryland, Douglas said in a letter to W. A. Graham that Delaware would continue to occupy a conservative position and would frown on any attempt to alienate "one portion of our glorious country from another." "It would give me great pleasure," he said, "to hear something of the sentiment of the Old North State. . . ."[6] A resolution that "in the opinion of the Assembly no person in favor of secession or a dissolution of the American Union ought to be elected to any office in the gift of the people of North Carolina" was introduced in the House on November 22. The vote was 69 to 46 to postpone action indefinitely. On that same date, Dennis D. Ferebee of Camden County introduced the following resolution in the House: First, that the United States was not a league or confederacy or compact between several sovereign states, but a government; Second, no State had the power to dissolve the federal-State relations, and nothing could dissolve those relations but revolution; Third, it was the duty of North Carolina under all circumstances, "and at all hazards," to protect, maintain, and defend, *in the Union,* all of the rights guaranteed to her citizens by the Constitution of the United States; and Fourth, that the election of Abraham Lincoln and Hannibal Hamlin by a sectional vote, however much to be deplored, was not a sufficient cause for a dissolution of the Union. His motion that the bill be laid on the table, printed, and referred to the Committee on Federal Relations, was lost. John F. Hoke of Lincoln County then offered the following resolution: First, the United States Constitution is a compact between sovereign and independent States and all powers not delegated are reserved to the States. One of the duties of State sovereignty is watching over the operations of the general government, protecting citizens from constitutional abuse, and securing for them strict fulfilment of the obligations imposed by the Constitution on the general government. Second, the people of North Carolina have the right to withdraw from the Union whenever a majority of them in convention assembled should decide that withdrawal is necessary for one or two reasons, viz., to protect their property or person from unconstitutional and oppressive legislation by the general government, or when the general government fails to fulfill its constitutional obligations.

This stronger, more secessionist resolution stated that in such an emergency the majority of the people, "acting through the organized authorites of the State, would be entitled to the sole and undivided allegiance of her citizens." No indication of any effort to take a vote on the Hoke resolution could be found. Augustus S. Merrimon of Buncombe County then offered the compromise resolution, viz.: Election of a sectional president and vice-president and "the fanatical, unwarranted, and dangerous policy of the Black Republican party" were to be "regretted and condemned." It was the sense of the General Assembly "that the rights of the people of this State under the Constitution of the United States shall be observed and enforced *in the Union* at all hazards and regardless of the consequences." In view of the general political condition of the country, the General Assembly recognized no cause which "rendered it wise . . . or necessary for this State now to send a delegate or delegates" to confer with the Southern States "in reference to any line of policy that looks to a dissolution of the Union or . . . the continuance of this State in the same." Merrimon warned, however, that the state "should be placed in such condition as to enable her to resist every encroachment upon the constitutional rights of her citizens." All of these resolutions were then laid on the table and ordered printed.

The Peyton H. Henry resolution was then introduced. It resolved that "in the opinion of the General Assembly, no person in favor of secession or dissolution of the American Union," ought to be elected to any office "in the gift of the people of North Carolina." Henry moved that his resolution be laid on the table, but on motion of Samuel J. Person of New Hanover County, it was postponed indefinitely.[7]

By November 29, 1860, Jonathan Worth reported "disunion influence" less potent in Raleigh than at the beginning of the legislature ten days earlier and expressed the hope that no action would be taken as to federal relations prior to Christmas. He wanted the Assembly to adjourn until after Lincoln had been inaugurated. If Lincoln should pledge to execute the Fugitive Slave Law, "and do it," he said he cared nothing about the question of squatter sovereignty. If Lincoln should adopt the southern doctrine that a State may disregard an act of Congress; if South Carolina, for example, seized the United States magazine and refused to pay duties or seized the public arms in the National Capitol Arsenal and Lincoln refused to coerce obedience, he could not enforce execution of the Fugitive Slave Law in the nullifying free States. In that case, Worth concluded, there would be virtually no Union to dissolve. Since then there would be no government, it would be expedient to establish one.

Worth was intensely devoted to the Union and viewed with alarm the progress of disunion sentiment in North Carolina and the South. He happened to be a winning candidate for the General Assembly in 1860. Having supported Bell and Everett in the election, he was one of the most determined opponents of the secession majority. Although he deeply regretted his membership in the Assembly, he thought it was wrong to resign in the midst of the crisis. He remained in his position and fought for the vain hope that North Carolina would stay in the Union. In his opposition to the convention, he canvassed Randolph County against it and was sustained by a large anti-convention majority. When the extra session opened in May, 1861, after the fall of Fort Sumpter, he continued to vote against a convention. When it was called, he declined to be a candidate, in spite of the wishes of his friends.

Reflection convinced Worth that war was inevitable, however, so he urged the men of Randolph County to volunteer and assist the South in presenting an unbroken front against the North, because he believed that was the only way the war could be shortened.

In a letter to J. J. Jackson, dated December 17, 1860, Worth discussed the three-hundred-thousand dollar appropriation for arms and South Carolina. South Carolina would become a paradise; through South Carolina, cotton would rule the world and "get plenty of Negroes from Africa," Worth said ironically, and the inhabitants of North Carolina "may possibly be allowed to attach ourselves as an humble dependency." Slavery, which he said was only a "pretext," was doomed if the South should set up a Southern Confederacy, because he said:

> With Canada in effect for her northern border from the Atlantic to the Pacific—all hating us, it is madness to think of anything else only to cut the throats of the negroes [sic] or have our own throats cut. I am very sorry that I am a member of the Assembly which I think contains less of patriotism than any like number of men ever assembled in this State since the close of the Revolution.
>
> Nearly all of the Democratic members desire to preserve the Union, but they are the rank and file and will all ultimately follow the leaders—at least, vote for the measures of Avery and Co.—all of which, openly or in disguise, look to a dissolution.

After the proposed Washington Conference "when we shall have called for a National Convention and it shall be refused, or shall have failed to accomplish a pacification," Worth indicated he would then recommend a dissolution of the Union.[8]

One original report titled "Union Meeting in Columbus County December 21st, 1860" was marked "To the Editor of the Raleigh Standard." A note on the back of the second page requested that the Editor "oblige . . . by handing this sheet when copied to Mr. N. S. Williamson [sic] member from Columbus."

"On short notice," eighty citizens of that county met in Whiteville on December 15, when R. H. McRacken "was called to the chair." Because of "bad weather," the meeting had to be postponed until December 21, when "over two hundred fifty persons, Whigs as well as Democrats," met in the courthouse. After the committee on resolutions was appointed and had retired, John Meares "was called out and made a good and patriotic appeal to his fellowmen in favor of the Union." The resolutions committee returned "at the close of his remarks" and offered the following resolutions, which were adopted: First, the Union is an inestimable blessing and the best form of government the world has ever seen. Every effort was urged to preserve the Union. Second, through prudence, moderation, and patriotism, the existing state of affairs could be settled, and the meeting expressed opposition to "immediate and separate secession." Third, President Buchanan's plan of reconciliation was approved and the message of Governor Ellis to the Assembly favoring secession and disunion was "entirely" disapproved. Fourth, the proceedings of the meeting should be forwarded to their senators and representatives in the Assembly and in the Congress of the United States "to be by them laid before their bodies."

Copies of the report were also to be sent to the *Wilmington Journal,* the *Wilmington Herald* and the *Raleigh Standard.*[9]

North Carolina was less responsible for the States' rights troubles prior to its secession than any of its Confederate neighbors. It was less fanatical, milder, more patient, and more concerned about concord than any selfish interests of its own. Because of this attitude, North Carolina was expected to share less than the other neighboring members of the Confederacy, which as early as the winter of 1860-61 were apparently on the verge of destruction. Sectional animosities, for which this State was not responsible and which it had not ceased to deplore, were expected in the process of alienating North and South to cause the slaveholding States to patronize the schools and manufactories of the South. Under this condition, whether the Union endured or failed, the neutral disposition was expected to benefit the people of North Carolina more than any other southern State.

Although the common school term was less than four months and the teacher could expect to earn less than one hundred dollars a year, Calvin H. Wiley, State Superintendent of Common Schools, believed that North Carolina had a better developed and more advanced system of common schools than any of its southern neighbors. Its geographic situation, climate, varied material resources, and the habit and character of its population were believed to give North Carolina decisive advantages over every southern competitor.[10]

Kenneth Rayner of Raleigh wrote to Thomas Ruffin on December 25 that he had returned from Hertford the previous Saturday where he "paid a hasty visit" to "attend to putting up my pork." He said he tried to sound out public opinion among the people there and was "mortified to find as far as I could ascertain that the feeling in that section,"

Hertford, Bertie, Gates, and adjacent counties, "was in a great measure in favor of the Union at any and all hazards." He said he had heard from several sources that the people who did not own slaves were swearing that they "would not lift a finger to protect rich men's negroes [*sic*]. You may depend on it, my dear judge," Rayner wrote, "that this feeling prevails to an extent you do not imagine."

He said the idea that there was antagonism between the poor people and the slaveholders had been "infused among the ignorant poor." He had thought previously, he explained, that if a convention was called in the State he would be a candidate in Hertford, but since he discovered the state of feeling there, he was doubtful whether he could be elected. Like Ruffin, Rayner was pro-Confederate and doubted that he could be elected in Hertford "unless I would pledge myself to the maintenance of the Union at all hazards, and under all circumstances. That I would not do." He said that although he was "a decided Union man in sentiment . . . ready to make any reasonable sacrifices and delays in order to save it . . . I have no hesitation in saying that I would surrender the Union rather than surrender the equality of my State with the other States, or our rights and property under the Constitution."[11] From Hamptonville in Yadkin County on December 28, "a friend" wrote to the pro-Union Whig *Fayetteville Observer* as follows:

> We are unanimous for the Union as it is. Some difference of opinion as to the *guarantees* we ought to insist upon. If there is cause for disunion now, it has existed for 8 years. But as the question is now placed upon us it ought to be settled now and forever; but let reason and forebearance prevail. . . .

On January 12, A. M. Bledsoe of Wake County introduced in the Senate a resolution designed to postpone conflict and containing three principal provisions: first, that the Assembly appeal to the President to withdraw the United States troops from the Atlantic and Gulf States and use his influence in favor of suspension of the revenue laws applicable in those States which had declared or may declare themselves out of the Union to prevent a collision between those States and the central government, and to allow for "an honorable and peaceful adjustment of pending difficulties between the North and the South"; second, that the Assembly appeal to the aforesaid States to "exercise in a spirit of conciliation all the forebearance consistent with their honor and safety" to prevent conflict between them and the federal government; and third, that the Assembly appeal to the governor to forward a copy of the resolution to the President and the governors of the aforesaid States.[12]

By mid-January, there were several opinions on the convention and secession question. Some members of the Assembly were in favor of caution and deliberation. They were opposed to precipitancy on a question so momentous, and wished to submit the question to the people. Some believed the Assembly had no power to submit this question to the people. Jonahan Worth said his constituents opposed a convention, that to call one would be "a species of revolution," and that he would vote for no bill that recognized the right of secession directly or indirectly. Some believed that there were indications of a returning sense of justice in the mind of the North and that time should be given for a complete reaction. Some who had been disunionist for several years believed their constituents would sustain them then and that the South should act as a unit and secede. Meanwhile a Raleigh correspondent to the *Fayetteville Observer* reported on January 17, that a resolution submitting the Crittenden plan to a vote of the people virtually "brought the crisis to an end." At the end of his article, the correspondent added:

> The disunion spirit is much less rampant here than it was a month ago, and grows tamer daily.

If the news from Washington is true, I presume the convention bills will be laid on the table and the General Assembly will address itself to ordinary legislation.[13]

When North Carolina sent envoys to Montgomery, Alabama, to attend the Confederate conference, even the Whig, pro-Confederate *Raleigh Register* immediately branded the action as absurd. Never had a more ridiculous embassy landed on a "foreign" shore, one editorial said, than was represented in the persons of North Carolina's "Envoys *Extraordinary* to the Congress of Seceders at Montgomery." Their treatment by the Congress was in conformity with the character of their mission as "observers." Admitted to seats in the open convention, they were excluded from the secret sessions. Described as "sorter so, and sorter not so" in a "state betweenity," these envoys were considered as political hermaphrodites to be known thereafter as the Hermaphrodite Embassy.

The Confederacy was far more optimistic than the *Register*. In a resolution ratified on February 8, it declared that North Carolina and the other Confederate States had "a common history, a common sympathy, a common honor, and a common danger," and that it was "the opinion and earnest desire of the Congress that . . . North Carolina should be united in government with these States." The Confederate Congress, therefore, resolved to receive with pleasure the North Carolina commissioners and hoped to "pursue such a course of action" as would "commend itself to, and induce . . . North Carolina especially" to unite with the seceded States "in such government as shall be formed by these States."

North Carolina had sent five representatives to the Washington Conference "to effect an honorable and amicable adjustment" of sectional difficulties "on the basis of the Crittenden resolutions as modified by the legislature of

Virginia." Since it was a part of the federal union, however, and had no right to send delegates to form a provisional or permanent government for the Confederate states, the Assembly appointed four commissioners to visit Montgomery for the same purpose the five delegates were sent to Washington.[14]

Senator Clingman told the Senate on February 20, that it was the duty of the United States government to withdraw all postal service from the States that had seceded, and that he regarded them as being as completely foreign states as was Great Britain. For the same reason that he would not vote money out of the public treasury to carry the mails through Great Britain, he said he could not vote to maintain the postal service in the South. He then proposed to suspend the mail in those States seceding from the Union.[15] He voted yea on the movement to expel the southern senators on March 14, when the motion was lost 10 to 24.[16] On February 23, letters from different parts of the State to the pro-southern *Raleigh Register* indicated that there was strong and growing sentiment for the Union and that "the convention would be overwhelmingly Union in complexion." Wake, which ranked second among the five leading slaveholding counties in North Carolina, expected to elect the Union ticket by the largest majority ever given any candidate in the county. Whigs and Democrats were "working together like beavers" and this was believed to be the case "in all quarters." If the Union was not saved it was to be from no lack of effort to preserve it in the Old North State.[17] The pro-Union Whig *Carolina Watchman* failed to regard the Confederate States as outside the Union, as Clingman had earlier. It said those States, despite their ordinances, seemed to be "nowhere recognized as out of the Union." They were counted in with Kansas to make thirty-four States, and entered into calculations "which look to the action of a majority of the States." The Confederate States did not seem to consider themselves as out of the Union, because they took full advantage of "Uncle Sam's money and name whenever and wherever" they could be of profitable use.[18] There were but a few counties in North Carolina in which the secession candidates for the State convention honestly avowed their principles. In New Hanover, Mecklenburg, and perhaps a few other counties they felt themselves strong enough to support immediate secession and disunion. Elsewhere they attempted to deceive the people under various pretenses. Even in Wake County, a leading secessionist stronghold, they operated under pretense. Even the *State Journal,* advocate of immediate secession, headed the disunion ticket as "State Rights Union Ticket."[19]

The general pattern of the pro-Union and pro-Confederate meetings was the same. The gathering was called to order and the chairman selected. A committee was immediately selected to write the resolutions. It retired promptly and during its absence a spellbinder (political orator) would address the audience. The final phase of the meeting was the reading and adopting of the resolutions.

An undated paper written after South Carolina seceded but before the secession of North Carolina, in some ways was typical of these reports. At Buffaloe in Moore County, J. B. Cole was "called to the chair." Addresses during the absence of the Committee on Resolutions were made by Dr. John McIver and James McIver, who condemned hasty action and opposed the dissolution of the Union, "untill [*sic*] all constitutional and honorable efforts to maintain our rights in the Union shall have been exhausted." The Committee resolutions were: first, that Lincoln's election was not sufficient cause for dissolution; second, that North Carolina need not necessarily secede because South Carolina did so; third, that this state should be determined "to resist encroachments on the Constitution and remain in the Union"; fourth, that the organization of the militia be approved;

fifth, that the meeting was not in favor of a State convention "untill [sic] the States which have passed personal liberty bills shall have had time and refused to repeal them"; sixth, that the Union could do without South Carolina and it was to be hoped that South Carolina would "be quietly let alone to experience the results of her head-strong wilfulness"; and seventh, that the meeting would not consent to a dissolution of the Union " 'till [sic] every honorbe [sic] constitutional and lawful effort to secure our rights has been exhausted."[20]

Alexander County citizens met in the courthouse on January 4, and resolved that "although frantic and bad men in the Northern States" had adopted "obnocious [sic] laws . . . calculated to arouse the indignation of the South . . ." redress was in the Union and not out of it. They looked to a dissolution of the Union as a last resort. Deeply regretting "the election of a sectional man to the presidency" they did not think it sufficient cause for a dissolution of the Union, "at least untill [sic] he has entered upon his office and indicated what the policy of his administration is to be as regards our rights and interests."

As men and as patriots, they said they had lived "happily and prosperously" in the Union and were determined to stand by it as long as they could do so without compromising their honor or sacrificing their interests. They said they believed the North Carolina policy was to stand firm, entirely aloof from influences of either North or South that would commit the State to any course of action, until circumstances indicated what course its interests required it to pursue. These resolutions were adopted "without a dissenting voice."[21]

A Hillsboro mass meeting adopted a similar but more detailed resolution which was reported on January 5, as follows:

First, that measures adopted in certain states since Lincoln's election raised questions as to whether the United

States Constitution was to continue in operation or be overthrown and annulled. Second, that while regretting the election decision, determined to observe vigilantly his administration, and prompt to resist encroachment on the rights and interests of slavery they perceived in the election no sufficient cause for the subversion and abandonment of the United States government. Third, that the government of the United States is a practical and limited government. The President is not sovereign but servant of the people with authority defined and restricted by the Constitution and laws, and checked and restrained by the Congress and courts. He was elected by a plurality because of division among the conservatives arrayed against him, and would not even be able to appoint his cabinet without consent of the conservative Senate. There was thus only a remote possibility of successful encroachment on rights in North Carolina during "the limited period of his administration." Fourth, that the State fugitive slave laws passed in the various States were unconstitutional and as a duty of justice and submission of the States to the Constitution the mass meeting demanded that they be replaced. Fifth, that secession was not an appropriate and adequate remedy for the injuries under which the Southern States were laboring. Loss of the North Carolina interest in the national accumulation of eighty years would be a sacrifice, except under pressure of "overruling necessity." Sixth, that it was considered wise and just to act, if possible, in concert and after consultation with the other slaveholding States, more especially Maryland, Virginia, Kentucky, and Missouri, who were suffering most from these grievances and standing as a barrier between the rest of the Southern States and "the enemies of their peace and safety beyond the frontier." Seventh, that reasonable time should be allowed and all remedies consistent with continuance of the Union exhausted before the abandonment of the Constitution. Eighth, that the Assembly make the necessary appropriations for the purchase of such supplies and arms as were necessary for any emergency that might arise. Ninth, that the resolution be published in the Hillsborough papers and transmitted to the representatives from that county to be laid before the General Assembly. It was signed by William H. Brown, chairman, and Dennis Heartt and C. E. Parish, secretaries.[22]

A Union mass meeting in Winston a few days later was presided over by R. L. Peterson, and C. L. Banner and A. J. Stafford were the secretaries. It also considered Lincoln's election insufficient cause for secession and the State fugitive slave laws unconstitutional. Secession, the resolution said, was an inadequate remedy to be entered into only after the "frontier" or border States had been consulted and sufficient time allowed to exhaust all remedies.[23]

The preamble to a resolution, dated January 10 and found among the Legislative Papers, charged the North with passing laws nullifying the fugitive slave law and refused to protect Southern property. Some States in the North were charged with "making every effort in their power to arm the slaves and incite them to rebellion and murder." Since election of Lincoln, it was charged, southerners had been murdered in pursuit of their slaves.

The resolution praised the United States Constitution as the work of patriots "and by far the best model for civil government wisdom and virtue . . ." ever devised "to protect minorities." All constitutional remedies should be "fairly tried and exhausted" before resort to extreme measures, it said, and Lincoln's election was not sufficient cause to dissolve the Union. It urged that the Assembly take immediate steps to reform the militia and arm "every free white man, of proper age, in the State," but that North Carolina remain in the Union, unless the federal government should administer principles inimical to its interests. In such case, it was recommended that North Carolina reserve the right to declare its independence and exist as a sovereign state or join the Confederacy. In a desperate effort to protect North Carolina slave property, the resolution also urged that the law be strengthened and that a court of claims be established in each State to inquire into and pay the value of slaves lost. There was no record that it was ever presented.[24]

At a meeting of "citizens of Howellsville District" held at the house of Shadrock Howell, Sr., on January 11, Tamer A. Rogers introduced the following resolution:

First, that they were "much gratified with the disposition now manifested by the free States toward the South. Their governors are recommending a repeal of all obnoxious laws in regard to fugitive slaves . . ." and that "from all we can see of their intentions, if we of the South will now act calmly and prudently, we see no reason why every difference should not be immediately settled. . . ." Second, that "we will contend for all our rights in the Union. . . . We can not give up the Constitution and Union until all efforts are made to get justice." The people of that section should "keep the peace and act kindly toward each other that a happy state of affairs may soon exist in all parts of this great country. . . ." Third, that the meeting condemned the citizens of South Carolina who were "trying to dissolve the Union . . . , break up the best form of government in the world's history, and destroy the only hope of the American people." Fourth, that the Union must be preserved and "we are opposed to the election of any county, State, or federal officer who is in favor of dissolving the Union."

To carry out their wishes, they requested that their representative in the Assembly be requested to vote for Bedford Brown for a seat in the United States Senate. Copies of the resolution were to be sent to the *Fayetteville Observer* and the North Carolina *Standard* for publication.[25] Meanwhile, the battle between the secessionists and the pro-Unionists and the pro-Union and pro-southern newspapers continued.

Early in January, following a program of speaking, cheering, and cannon firing, the secessionists in Wilmington raised a "lone-star flag." Since cannon firing was going on all over the South, the pro-Unionists suggested that perhaps the South was burning up too much powder in advance, "the only effect of which, just now, is to make it necessary to buy more ammunition—from the North."[26] By April, the pro-Unionist groups were accusing pro-Confederates of forming secret organizations in North Carolina, but they branded this insinuation as absurd and ridiculous. They said the know-nothing or dark lantern party was the only secret political organization "we ever heard of in the State." The pro-Confederate *State Journal* said the *Standard* was working with the secret organization, the debris of the party whose members it stigmatized in 1860 as submissionists for holding the same opinion the *Standard* then held.[27]

Obviously, these newspapers were sometimes right and sometimes wrong. The *Semi-Weekly Raleigh Register* said that North Carolina's interests did not lie with the "Cotton State Confederacy," because in confederacy with them its voice would be lost and its interests disregarded. The interests of North Carolina were identical with those of Tennessee, Virginia, Kentucky, and Maryland, the newspaper asserted, "and if she leaves the present Union, it will be in company with these States that she will go."[28] Yet the contrast between the upper and lower South was best revealed in the difference between North Carolina, which was last, and South Carolina, which was first to secede.

With this reference to the question of secession, some consideration will now be given to the various peace efforts. That the nomination of Lincoln was the event that disturbed the peace is indicated in a letter from Paul C. Cameron of

Hillsboro, plantation owner and slaveholder in Mississippi as well as North Carolina, to Thomas Ruffin. On Friday, October 12, Cameron wrote Ruffin that he was "growing very anxious about the presidential election." He pointed out that although the election was "near at hand" there was hardly any more "light" as to the results than there had been two months before. "With the 15 Southern States . . . the 2 [sic] Pacific States, and a fusion in Pennsylvania, all may go well with our ticket, but my belief now is that the 'Black Republicans' will get the Government into their hands."[29] Thus, many prominent persons may have believed Lincoln would be elected from the beginning. The unpopularity of Lincoln in the slaveholding States led South Carolina to secede, and the peace movement followed. Since secession threats preceded secession, it was possible for the neighboring States to use their influence to keep South Carolina in the Union.

A resolution was introduced in the North Carolina Senate to appoint Thomas Ruffin of Alamance, Weldon N. Edwards of Warren, William A. Graham of Orange, and William N. H. Smith of Hertford County, State commissioners, to report to the South Carolina legislature which was then in session, to consider the question of secession. They were to report that although North Carolina "fully appreciates the patriotic considerations that have called them together, and feels all the sympathy and respect which historic renown, common interests, and their relations as a sister coterminous State should inspire," they would appeal to South Carolina to suspend any action by which secession from the Union would be accomplished. They were to ask the South Carolina legislature to await a common consultation of all of the Southern States, the results of which would be submitted to the people of the several States concerned before final action. The commissioners would also be authorized to proceed "to any Southern sister States," express similar sentiments, and appeal to them to forebear action that might lead to separation from the Union. Their pay was to be six dollars a day and they were to be granted the same travel allowance as members of the North Carolina General Assembly. The bill was lost 22 to 19 on December 10.[30]

On January 14, Josiah Turner of Orange County offered to amend an engrossed resolution from the House on Federal relations to read:

> That the Hons. Thos. Ruffin and William A. Graham be and . . . are hereby appointed Commissioners to visit the President of the United States and the Governor of South-Carolina, and communicate to them the sentiment of the Assembly, as expressed in these resolutions.

However, Lottie W. Humphrey of Onslow County moved to table both resolution and amendment.[31] On the following day, Turner introduced the resolution again and it was read the first time and passed. These resolutions provided that the commissioners appointed "speak for a restoration of peace and harmony to the whole country."[32]

Virginia requested that the General Assembly appoint and send five commissioners "to Washington City" to confer with commissioners appointed by Virginia and other States "in an effort to restore the Constitution in the spirit in which it was formed." In response to this request, a resolution was introduced, providing for amendment of the resolutions presented in the United States Senate by Senator John J. Crittenden to make them apply to territory that may be acquired in the future by the United States government. The North Carolina resolution expressed the opinion that such an amendment would be satisfactory to the people of North Carolina, but although North Carolina was seeking peace, "no compromise embracing less than the principles of said resolution" would be satisfactory to the South. With this resolution was the pencil copy of a resolution which provided for selection of four commissioners from each house to be sent to Washington and four from each house to be sent to Montgomery, Alabama, in the interests of peace. It was dated January 20, 1861, and marked "adopted," but resolutions to this effect were not approved in the North Carolina General Assembly until nine days later. On that date a resolution was adopted appointing Thomas Ruffin, D. M. Barringer, David S. Reid, John Morehead, and George Davis to attend the Washington Conference, and David L. Swain, R. W. Ransom, and John L. Bridgers to attend the Montgomery Conference. A resolution adopted by the first extra session of the Assembly on May 8 reappointed the latter delegations to meet with Union officials in Washington and Confederate officials in Montgomery, respectively. The Montgomery Conference passed a resolution on February 8, that the Congress "shall receive with pleasure the commissioners from the State of North Carolina, and hope to pursue such a course of action as shall commend itself to, and induce the State of North Carolina speedily to unite in our councils and in such Government as shall be formed by these States." This resolution was passed before North Carolina had called a convention to consider secession, but Confederate leaders were familiar with the efforts of the States' rights party to join the Confederacy. The Confederacy, like the Union, had considerable trouble with North Carolina, but North Carolina tried to cooperate, because the State convention selected ten delegates to attend the Confederate Congress at Richmond on July 20,[33] and aided the Confederacy in other ways.

Meanwhile, the North Carolina representatives in the Senate and House of the United States Congress were struggling with the problem of peace. Representative Warren Winslow, on January 22, "by unanimous consent, presented to the House the proceedings of a meeting by the citizens of Columbia, North Carolina, in reference to the condition of the country." It was promptly "laid on the table."[34] Representative James M. Leach asked and attained unanimous consent to present to the House "the proceedings and actions of a very large meeting held in the Town of Lexington, North Carolina, upon the present crisis." The Lexington citizens had approved resolutions designed to lead to "a settlement of our national troubles . . . based on the Crittenden propositions." Leach urged the House to read and consider the resolution "with the hope that North Carolina might be in some degree instrumental in effecting an adjustment of our difficulties."[35] When the House voted to provide militia for the District of Columbia on January 29, in announcing his negative vote, Leach said:

> My voice is still for peace and I persist in the determination heretofore formed, to give no vote which would increase sectional excitement.[36]

Winslow said he was willing to exert all of his power to effect a suitable settlement to preserve Union, but in his judgment "no patched up compromise, no alleviating and palliating remedy" was either just or prudent. He said he did not subscribe to the dogma that the Union should be preserved "at all hazards." With reference to the reluctance with which North Carolina ratified the original Constitution of the United States, he said North Carolina was thus reluctant because it feared the consequences "which have sadly been realized." When it did come into the Union it came with loyal purposes to adhere to its obligations, and would then take the course which her honor, interest and obligation to the other States justified.[37]

James M. Leach, in a State of the Union message on February 7, said the problems could be worked out and demanded that it be done. Unless there was an immediate return to the obligations of the Constitution, however, and a recognition of the equality of all of the States and a guarantee of the rights of the South by the people of the North, he said peace could not be preserved. He pleaded with the House to join him and so legislate as to bring the rebellious States back into the Union.

The decline and fall of the Democratic party and the consequent ability of the Republicans to organize and get control of the government was due to the repeal of the Missouri Compromise, he said, but he added :

> . . . in my judgment there can be no warrant for it (secession) in the Constitution . . . no foundation for it, as derived in any way from that instrument. If a State has a constitutional right to secede, the Constitution of the United States would be subject to the will and control of every State in the Union . . . the mere creature, not only of the States, but . . . of every one of them, for it could be destroyed at any time by any State.

Even if secession were constitutional, he said he could not see how it could be a remedy for the complaints of the South and that it was "certainly a matter of profoundest regret" that the cotton States, following the lead of South Carolina, "saw fit to withdraw from the Union." He listed the main complaints against the North as: First, "your [the North's] president's encroachments upon the rights of the South, as manifested in your personal liberty laws." Second, the exclusion of the South with its slave property from the territories "in derogation of the decision of the United States Supreme Court in the Dred Scott case." Third, "your denial of property in slave upon the quibble that they are 'persons only.'" Fourth, the threatened interference with slavery in the District of Columbia and in the forts, arsenals, and dock yards. Fifth, the "irrepressible conflict" dogma, of eventually striking down slavery in the states. Sixth, "your triumph as a sectional party on the one idea of hostility to slavery in the election of sectional candidates, who on account of their sectional views, failed to receive one electoral vote in fifteen of the States of the Union. . . ."

Leach proposed that all of the problems could be solved if the North would accept the Crittenden Compromise "proposed by our country's greatest living statesman." What was needed were such guarantees as would satisfy the border States and induce them not only to remain in the Union, but to exert their good offices as mediators between the extremes of both sections. By following this course and by conciliation, kindness, and assurances that the rights of these border States would be protected in the Union, Leach believed the border States would "endeavor to influence those [seceded] States to remain in the Union, but if a coercive policy is adopted, all is lost."

Urging that the Crittenden-Bigler proposition "but be submitted to the voters of this Union," he concluded, "and . . . it will be adopted." The *hearts* of the *people* are right! It is the hearts of the politicians that are wrong.[38]

On the following day, Representative William N. H. Smith delivered a less compromising State of the Union speech in which he said there was still time to make "a peace offering" to North Carolina. He said he did not know what would be the policy of North Carolina, but would soon know, because a convention was about to be called there, and, like Leach, he approved the Crittenden Compromise. He said it would permit the North to control more than three-fourths of the territory of the United States as free soil, and the South what was left. He contended that slaves may be persons, and they may be property. They were recognized as *persons* when counted as part of the population upon which representation is based, and as property when they were required to be surrendered by the States into which they had escaped while fleeing from their owners. He explained this concept as follows:

> . . . They are not mere chattels, but also moral and responsible beings. . . . Slaves are punishable for the crimes they commit. The master has only such control over the

person of his slaves as is necessary for the purpose of securing the full enjoyment of his services. They are regarded as persons within the protection of the laws which are thrown as safeguards around human life. But they are at the same time in subjection to others to whom their labor belongs. There is no incompatibility between the two. Obedience and protection are their correlative duties and rights.

The South, he said, was willing to accept less than one-fourth of the territory of the United States "in which to practice slavery," but wanted a constitutional right to it to be written into the Constitution. It insisted on both of these conditions to establish peace and that the nation might develop a common understanding of the respective rights and duties of each section. He indicated, however, that this might be a barren right, by adding:

. . . We may be unable to retain ultimately a single foot of slaveholding territory, but we shall have established a principle of equality of rights by which the popular mind will be quieted and a fertile cause of strife removed. We may bring to a peaceful conclusion embittered controversies which have impelled us to the brink of national dissolution and restore among alienated States such relations of amity and good will as will bind them in harmony ere the introduction of this element of sectional discord, at the admission of Missouri into the Union.

"Far better" would it have been, Smith said, "if separation and division must come, and the States can not remain in Union longer, that they part in amity and peace."[39]

The major peace effort was the Washington Conference which was in session from February 4 to February 29. A resolution was introduced in the House which nominated Weldon N. Edwards, K. Rayner, and Edward G. Reid to meet with delegates from Virginia and other Southern States "at Washington City" on February 4 "to devise some mode of settlement of our national difficulties."[40] Paul C. Cameron wrote Ruffin that he hoped he would have fine weather for his trip to Washington and told him to "keep your eye on those who talk about a 'Central Republic'" and to "ask only what is right, and submit to nothing that is wrong." Cameron told Ruffin that he was not going to Washington "to make a good bargain for the South, but to obtain justice," yet he added:

> Exclude the Negro of all degrees of blood from the ballot box.

> I fear nothing can be accomplished and that we must take our place with our Sister States of the South.[41]

It has already been noted that North Carolina had a peace delegation in Washington and Montgomery at the same time. Various resolutions were introduced in the Assembly, urging conciliation. An undated resolution, marked "adopted as amended," and found among the Legislative Papers for 1860-61, urged

> That the Commissioners to Montgomery be, and they are hereby instructed, to act as mediators and use every effort possible to affect a reconciliation between the North and South and thus endeavor to restore the Union which formerly existed between the American States.

This resolution and others that the Montgomery Commissioners be instructed "to act only as mediators" indicate that the Commissioners to the Confederate Conference at Montgomery were sent only as observers.[42] The Montgomery Conference differed from the Washington Conference in several ways. It was called not to discuss the hazards of secession and secure southern rights in the Union, but to abandon the Union, erect a new political structure, and organize a southern government. There were representatives only from South Carolina, Georgia, Alabama, Mississippi, Florida, and Louisiana. Its main function was to write a constitution for the Confederate States, choose the provisional president and vice-president, and to serve as a provisional legislature for the new government pending the regular congressional elections. Obviously, the North Carolina commissioners could not participate in such activities.

At the Washington Convention, our commissioners were more active. The governor was required to send each commissioner his commission and to give all of them formal instructions. They were authorized "to exercise the duties and powers of each appointment" according to their best judgment and discretion.[43] Upon arrival in Washington, they were issued certificates by the Conference Convention, signed by John Tyler, President of the Convention.[44]

By the end of the Convention, there were representatives from twenty-one States. They proposed the following seven amendments to the Constitution of the United States, to be presented to the new Congress then in session:

First, that slavery be prohibited north of the thirty-six degree, thirty minute parallel, but that it continue undisturbed south of that line. Second, that no territory be acquired by the United States, except by discovery and for naval and commercial stations, depots, and transit routes, without approval of a majority of the senators in both slaveholding and free States, within the two-thirds majority vote necessary for ratification of the treaty. Third, that the Congress not have power to abolish, regulate, or control slavery in any State. Fourth, that Article IV, Section 2, Paragraph 3 of the United States Constitution not be construed to prevent any States by legislature, judiciary, or administrative agents, from forcing delivery of fugitive slaves. Fifth, that the foreign slave trade was forever prohibited and that the Congress pass laws to prevent importation of slaves, coolies, and persons held to service or labor, into the United States. Sixth, that the Constitution not be amended without consent of all of the States. Seventh, that when an officer whose duty is to arrest a fleeing slave is prevented from doing so by violence or intimidation and the owner is thus deprived of the slave, Congress should pass legislation providing that the United States should pay to the owner the full value of his slave.

On March 5, John M. Morehead, one of the delegates to the Convention, wrote Thomas Ruffin, also a member, that he regretted very much to see from the published votes of the Convention that North Carolina had voted against all seven proposals, except the third and fourth. He said he was satisfied that the people of the State would pass them all by a majority of six to one and that he was "exceedingly gratified . . . that you favored each of them."[45] Edward Sturdwick had already predicted on February 2 that the peace convention would fail "The Cotton States" he said, "will hardly accept any arrangement made by the border, free, and slave States . . . if the Union can not be reconstructed, let not its dismemberment be stained with blood."[46]

While the peace convention was going on, the Congress was also in session. In the convention and the Congress, every member was doing all that he could to maintain peace, but both major factions of the convention and both major factions in the Congress were determined to accept peace only on their own terms. The Congressmen from North Carolina fought valiantly for the Union, but perhaps with equal valor for the South. They all seemed determined to support secession only as a last resort, but they differed as to what they would tolerate and what condition they would consider as the last resort.

On the opening day of the convention, Senator Wiliam L. Clingman expressed grave concern about the possibility that the slaves might be liberated and left as free Negroes to live in the communities where they were held as slaves. There were less than four million slaves, but Clingman asserted that it was sometimes said that they were worth four billion dollars. "This, I suppose, is true," he said, "but that is only a portion of the pecuniary loss, if we are deprived of them." He said that in the North, for example, if the horses and working cattle, vehicles, and working utensils were removed, the lands themselves would have little value. Liberation of the slaves in the South would likewise be so great a loss that financial ruin would be inevitable. Even this would not be the greatest evil. Instead it would be the infusion into southern society of a large free Negro population and "the social destruction of our society" by this population that would be most dreadful. Yet, again stressing the value of the slaves, he said:

. . . The negroes [sic] of the South are, in most of the States, worth more than the lands. Suppose there was a proposition now to abolish land titles through the free States, that, if adopted, would produce immense mischief; but in addition suppose there were to be transferred to those States a free negro [sic] population, equal to half their own . . . would not the people of those States at once rise in rebellion against such measures?

Clingman said that the English newspapers could not understand the United States, because "they draw their ideas altogether from opinions expressed in the North." Then he added:

. . . Our slave property exceeds the national debt in England in value. How long could a ministry stand that was for abolition of the national debt?

All that was produced in the North could be produced in the South "in the greatest of abundance" as far as agriculture was concerned, he said, and the South might manufacture everything on earth that is needed. If the whole cotton crop "were detained at home," Clingman said he did not believe it would affect the ultimate prosperity of the South.

He was addressing the North throughout his speech, a large portion of which population he said believed the North was wrong. He said the industrial population would suffer more than the South in a war, and pointed out three alternatives which he considered progressively less commendable: peace settlement, recognition of peaceful separation, or war.

Not only were the North and South badly divided, but the South itself was divided. If this had not been true—if the South had not been divided in 1860—all of the South would have seceded. It was North-South division on three issues that Clingman said would lead to war between the States. They were the Union Pacific Bill "by which we have undertaken . . . to build three railroads at a cost of one hundred twenty million dollars . . . , the tariff bill, likely to be adopted, which passed the House by a large vote, containing most iniquitous provisions for the benefit of particular classes," and the Homestead Bill. Clingman objected to the latter bill on the ground that the United States was giving up public property while the treasury was bankrupt and the United States was borrowing money. In summarizing his objections to these legislative proposals, Clingman said the northeast would get the tariff, the northwest would get the benefit of the Pacific railroad and the Homestead Bill, and the "Republicans or Abolitionists" would "get anti-slavery."[47]

In resuming these arguments in another State of the Union message on February 7, Senator Leach was still anti-secessionist, because he believed secession an inadequate remedy, but blamed the Republicans.

Sectional difficulties could be settled by representatives of the American people assembled in Congress. The Constitution could be preserved, he said, peace and harmony restored, and adjustment made on a fair basis, but "honorable alike to all sections."

Leach considered the difficulties as resulting generally from failures of the Constitution which he said "no longer spreads its peaceful and protecting shelter over thirty-three

States . . . six have . . . shot proudly from their orbits.
. . . They have left the great sisterhood and are now essaying
to set up for themselves." Active agitation by both North
and South, often led by wicked and unscrupulous demigogues
had succeeded in getting into power. By the abuse of this
power they had "sent all over the land . . . speeches, circulars,
and pamphlets, misrepresentations of the real feelings, opinions, and sentiments of the people of one section towards
those of the other." He admitted that it was the Democrats
who repealed the Missouri Compromise which together with
corruption and reckless extravagance "of the present Democratic administration" led to organization and victory of the
Republican party. "Representatives of the North," he said,
nevertheless, "these troubles have been brought on by your
gradual but persistent encroachments upon the rights of
the South."

The resulting problems were referred to collectively as
"sectionalism." These sectional difficulties could be settled
by representatives of the American people in Congress assembled, but he added:

> . . . The responsibility of settling our difficulties rests
> mainly upon you, gentlemen of the Republican party, who
> are now dominant in both Houses of the Congress, and
> who have recently attained power and are about to assume
> the administration of the General Government. And you
> should come to the rescue promptly; for it is in vain to
> talk about delay until after the inauguration of your Presi-
> dent. I greatly fear it will then be too late.

From Clingman's point of view, the general problem
seems to have been sectionalism, and in order to effect a
solution North and South would have to sit down and bargain; but since the North was more responsible than the
South, Clingman seemed to think that it should to a large
extent submit to the wishes of the South, and so "legislate
as to bring them [the seceded States] back" into the Union.

Dismissing the secession alternative as entirely unsatisfactory, he concluded:

> . . . I will not consume my time arguing the question of secession further than to say that, in my judgment, there can be found no warrant for it in the Constitution, and no foundation for it, as derived in any way from that instrument. If a State has a constitutional right to secede, then the Constitution of the United States would be subject to the will and control of every State in the Union. It could be destroyed at any time by any State.
>
> I can not see how secession, even if constitutional, can afford any remedy for the grievances of the South. . . . This action of the cotton States was . . . unjustifiable and unwise. . . . They have shown themselves wanting in respect for their sister slave States; espcially when it is remembered that but for their withdrawal . . . there would have been a declared majority in *both Houses of Congress* against the incoming administration. . . .[48]

Senator Clingman placed all hope in favorable legislation, and absolutely no hope in secession. Representative Burton Craige, "the tallest man in the House," apparently rejected all alternatives except secession the next day, because he said: "I have no hope that anything will result from that 'peace congress.' "[49]

Craige not only conceived of amicable relations between the Confederacy and the United States as desirable, but agreed that the President should acknowledge the independence of the Confederacy and receive an envoy, ambassador, or commissioner from that government. He moved that his resolution be referred to the Committee on Foreign Affairs, to which it was referred on February 11.[50]

Thus, no satisfactory solution to these problems could be found. Some of the results of this failure are contained in the following chapter.

Chapter Seven

States' Rights and Secession

NORTH CAROLINA was never, not even before 1860, entirely pro-Union. It would be hard to say how much pro-Union, neutral, or secessionist sentiment existed in the State at any time prior to 1861, but North Carolina was badly divided on this question. However, secession was regarded as a possibility. A resolution was introduced in the Senate on November 27, 1860, with reference to secession talk in North Carolina and other States and urging that our senators and representatives, "while North Carolina is a member of the Confederacy" (the United States), apply to the current session of the Congress for North Carolina's share of the public lands "and that they do all in their power" to obtain them.[1] ". . . Our political surroundings make me sad and apprehensive. I think we are in imminent peril of a national dissolution. Indeed," said Metthias E. Manly, "I can hardly say a hope is left that it will be avoided." Writing on December 2, shortly after the 1860 election, he said that the election of Lincoln under the circumstances would lead to grave problems if the Lincoln administration should insist on regarding slaves in the South as a moral tint which it was its duty to eradicate. In that case, he felt that North Carolina would be compelled to secede from the Union. If the Lincoln administration had no such purpose, or having such purpose, would abandon it, Manly could see no reason why the Union could not continue intact. What Manly feared was that President Lincoln and his cabinet would not only *have* such purpose, but would not abandon it.[2]

This uncertainty and doubt continued in 1861. Bills authorizing or empowering the governor to call a convention of the people of the State to determine whether North Carolina should or should not secede, frequently got no further than the Committee or were tabled. However, newspapers were changing policy. The New Bern *Progress,* theretofore anti-secessionist, supported immediate secession on January 26, yet the *Raleigh Register* could still report:

> We regret that the *"Progress"* has come out as an advocate of separate secession by North Carolina. So far from thinking now that separate secession is the true policy, we are more and more of the opinion that it is the very worst that can be pursued.[3]

As time passed, this passion for secession was intensified. A public meeting of Halifax, Martin, and Edgecombe County citizens was held on November 15, 1860, at Palmyra. It was resolved that

> It is the sense of this meeting that in the event of the sovereign State of Georgia following South Carolina in her secession movement, we favor the withdrawal of North Carolina from the Federal Union.

To this committee resolution, the following amendment was offered in the general meeting:

> That in the event Alabama and Mississippi join South Carolina and Georgia in a secession movement, we favor the withdrawal of North Carolina from the Federal Union.

The resolution was then passed with only one dissenting vote.[4] At a meeting of citizens of Wilson and adjoining counties on November 24, it was resolved that the election of Abraham Lincoln and Hannibal Hamlin to the Presidency and Vice-presidency of the United States "ought not to be, and will not be, submitted to," that North Carolina had a right to secede, and in any emergency, "it was the proper remedy." It was signed by Joshua A. Barnes, Chairman, and B. H. Bardin, Secretary.[5]

A meeting of citizens in the town hall in Fayetteville on this date passed a resolution listing some of the complaints that they had against the President-elect and the North as follows: repeated aggression of a purely sectional party on the rights of the South, "total disregard of the Fugitive Slave Law," and election of Abraham Lincoln. This, they said, required the Assembly and the people to make immediate preparation for the defense of the rights of North Carolina. The Constitution is a compact of "sovereign independent States," they explained, and the right of secession exists under two conditions: when it is necessary to protect the property of persons from oppressive legislation, and when the Congress fails to recognize and secure to the Southern States their rights under the Constitution.[6] A report of a Sampson County meeting held at Clinton on November 25 was sent directly to Thomas J. Faison, a member of the Senate, then in session in Raleigh. It expressed a strong belief in State sovereignty and the right of a State to secede when a majority of the people in convention agree that there has been a violation of the federal contract. With secession clearly within the scope of its designs, the report urged a State convention, reform of the militia, and "appropriation of a sum (of money) sufficient to arm every free white man in the State." Catawba County citizens met in the courthouse on December 8. Lincoln had been chosen by the exclusive suffrage of Northern States, they reasoned, because of "his declared opinions . . . that slavery is a sin and crime and avows the purpose to abolish slavery and place the negro [sic] upon an equality with the white man." They resolved that North Carolina was a sovereign State and has a right to withdraw from the Union when in her opinion the rights guaranteed her by the Constitution have been violated by any of the States "or any coordinate branch of the General Government." Yet upon withdrawal of any State from the Union "no power exists under the Constitution to coerce or subjugate such seceding State."[7] By the time the Secession Manifesto was issued in Washington and signed by 29 of the 120 congressmen from the South in mid-December, they considered the arguments "exhausted." The Manifesto, dated December 14, 1860, reads as follows:

> The arguments are exhausted. All hope of relief in the Union through the agency of committees, congressional legislation, or constitutional amendments, is extinguished; and we trust the South will not be deceived by appearances or the pretence [sic] of new guarantees. . . . The Republicans are resolute in their purpose to grant nothing that will or ought to satisfy the South. We are satisfied the honor, safety, and independence of the Southern people require the organization of a Southern confederacy—a result to be obtained only by separate State secession—that the primary object of each slaveholding State ought to be its speedy and absolute separation from a Union with hostile States.[8]

Orange County citizens, in a meeting on December 26 in the courthouse at Hillsboro, resolved to recommend to the current session of the Assembly the calling of a convention of the people "to take under consideration the alarming state of public affairs" and to determine for North Carolina the "time, mode, and measure of redress for existing wrongs." Adopted by a large majority, it was signed by William H. Brown, Chairman of the meeting.[9]

"A large and enthusiastic meeting" of citizens of Smithville in Brunswick County "irrespective of party" was held on December 29. Colonel George Wortham of Granville, largest slaveholding county in the state, delivered "a strong Southern speech." The contents of the resolutions passed in this meeting could not be found, but there are indications

that there was a resolution. The proceedings were ordered
furnished "to each of our representatives in the General
Assembly and . . . to the *Wilmington Journal* and the
Raleigh State Journal with a request to publish—and . . .
to be copied by all papers friendly to Southern independ-
ence." The meeting then adjourned "with three cheers for
Secession, and three cheers, long and loud, for the *Old North
State*."[10]

In a speech before the House on January 29, Representative Warren Winslow said that the North had threatened the
State with constitutional modes by which it could, and thereafter meant to, extinguish slavery as a system. Meanwhile,
slavery had become "so interlocked and interwoven with
our institutions that the destruction of the parasite would
be death to the tree it clings to." He said the North refused
to write into the Constitution an amendment prohibiting
slavery above the thirty-six degree, thirty minute parallel
on the grounds that the North would have been making no
concession, since slavery could never obtain a permanent
footing there. Then, accusing the North of denying the
South equality in the territories, he concluded that the
North sought this to reduce the South "to the position of a
degraded people." The North then "presented before the
country" a ticket "strictly sectional," availing itself of "unhappy differences between North and South." He said the
North thus succeeded in establishing an administration, submission to which without further guarantees, would leave
the South a conquered people, under foreign domination.
He might have added, however, that the South had tried to
"avail itself of unhappy differences," but apparently had lost.

"You say that slavery can never go into Mexico," Winslow told the House, "and that we stand upon an abstrac-
tion." The South did maintain the right to takes its slaves to
Mexico, he said, and concluded:

It is a fancied or real right. If the former, you admit it can do you no harm, can not affect your policy or . . . ours. If real, then the deprivation of it to us is a great wrong, and according to our notions, the surrender of it, on our part, and the prohibition of it on yours, would reduce us to the condition of a degraded people and work a forfeiture of our self respect.

Moreover, Winslow said that if bloodshed resulted, the Union could not be reconstructed.[11]

From his first entrance into politics, Thomas Ruffin said he had "been an advocate of the right of secession." In his judgment, he said in the House of Representatives on February 20, the time had come when all of the Southern States still in the Union and recognizing slavery should, through secession, seek outside the Union "such associations as would afford them the protection denied them within it." Praising Jefferson Davis, President, and Alexander H. Stephens, Vice-President of the Confederacy, Ruffin emphasized that he was "free to confess" . . . and to "proclaim with pride" that his sympathies were with the South and "in peace or war, they shall continue with the South. . . ."

The people of North Carolina and other States still in the Union had the alternative of remaining in the Union, which Ruffin termed submission, or secession. Since North Carolina was closest to the seceded States, it might become the first State from which Lincoln would requisition troops. The union of the States having been dissolved, North Carolina would select its own associates, but its interests, sympathies, and destiny were with the South. Ruffin refused to discuss a middle confederacy, because, he said, it did not have "even the merit of Southern origin."

He admitted that there were differences of opinion among southern men as to when the time would come to leave the Union, but he believed that the time had arrived, the nation was in the midst of crisis, and that the sooner the remaining Southern States seceded the better. He said it would be fortunate for North Carolina if it could withdraw before the tax bill before the Congress became law. The passage of the tariff bill and the gigantic project for construction of three Pacific railroads, he said, would "entail upon this country an enormous debt" and "render the Union no longer desirable for the South," under any circumstances that were likely to occur. It was far better to be in "a new confederacy," he said, "where we can have an economical government."[12]

By the middle of March the secession spirit had reached Wilson, where a southern rights meeting was held in the county courthouse on March 16. It was resolved that it was the duty of North Carolina as well as every other slave-holding State "to detach itself from the old confederation whose constitution has been violated by a majority of the States composing it . . . and join the brotherhood of States at the South."[13] There was also talk of a southern plot to assassinate President Lincoln.[14] Citizens assembled in the courthouse at Tarboro on April 2, formed a county southern rights organization, and elected William Thigpin chairman and W. B. Smith secretary, on motion of John L. Bridgers. It voted that the proceedings of the next meeting which was to be held on April 25 or 26 were to be submitted to the county newspapers and that the "Southern rights" news-papers of the State be requested to copy.[15] By that time there were Southern Rights Executive Committees in eight dis-tricts in the State.[16] Before the end of the month, the Union leaders throughtout North Carolina had "all come over o the cause of resistence."[17]

These acts were the first of a series of rapidly occurring events which alienated North Carolina from the Union and caused it to draw closer to the South. The second series began with the Washington request for troops to defend the Union.

On April 15, Simon Cameron, Secretary of War, wired Governor John W. Ellis of North Carolina:

> Call made on you by to-night's mail for two regiments of military for immediate service.

To this message Ellis replied on the same day:

> Your dispatch is received; and if genuine, which its extraordinary character leads me to doubt, I have to say in reply that I regard the levy of troops made by the administration for the purpose of subjugating the States of the South as a violation of the Constitution and a gross usurpation of power. I can be no party to this wicked violation of the laws of the country and to this war upon the liberties of a free people. *You can get no troops from North Carolina.*
>
> I will reply more in detail when your 'call' is received by mail.[18]

The Assembly seemed to be afraid that the governor might not take what it considered the "necessary action" leading to a convention, but throughout the latter part of 1860 and the early part of 1861, there was an ardent nucleus of support for various "necessary" measures. On December 5, a resolution was introduced in the House, providing that if any State dissolved its connection with the general government and any attempt was made by the general government to coerce such a State, North Carolina would "make common cause with the State so seceding." A similar resolution was introduced on January 10. The Supreme Court requested the Assembly to express its opinion as to the right or power of the Assembly under the State constitution to call a convention of the people of the State "for every purpose" without a two-thirds vote of both Houses. The House agreed to submit this opinion to the Court on December 11 and sent the House resolution to the Senate, requesting that the Senate concur. On January 1, Governor Ellis was authorized to issue a proclamation to all sheriffs to open the polls on February 28 to consider action to be taken concerning grievances of North Carolina as a member of the federal union. Each sheriff was required to make separate returns, one to be deposited in the office of the county clerk and the other to be transmitted to the General Assembly. The Assembly requested Ellis to "cause the publication in all the newspapers of the State" of the act providing for a convention of the people of North Carolina and passed on January 1, and to furnish the sheriffs of each county fifty handbills containing notice of the time of the election proposed to be held. Finally Senate Resolution 190, which was tabled on February 27, resolved: first, that the territories of the United States belonged to the several States composing the Union, held as their joint and common property; second, that the Congress was the joint agent and representative of the States; and third, that when congressional legislation deprived North Carolina citizens of the right of migrating with their slave property into any of the territories of the United States, the Governor was "hereby required to issue a proclamation commanding the sheriffs of the respective counties" to conduct elections to determine whether a convention of the people would be held. The delegates to any convention called were to have the same pay and allowances of assemblymen and to take action only on "such grievances as affect North Carolina as a member of the Confederacy." The convention was to be composed of the same number of delegates from each county as the total number of representatives. Such ordinances as might by enacted by the convention were to be ratified by the Assembly.[19] The hard core of "fire-eaters" who had struggled with these problems against the indifferent wait-and-see attitude of the neutrals and pro-Unionists thus had prepared the way for quick action when the Assembly convened on May 1. Because President Lincoln requested that North Carolina provide seventy-five thousand troops and "the high handed act of tyrannical outrage" by the federal government, two days after Ellis received this call, he issued a call for a special session of the General Assembly to meet on May 1. On the opening day of the first extra session, the Assembly ratified legislation which required the Governor to issue a proclamation ordering election of delegates to a State convention to be held on May 13. The convention was to consist of one hundred twenty delegates, each county entitled to the same number as it was entitled to in the House of Commons under the last apportionment.[20] The sheriff sent out certificates of election to the candidates from May 13 to May 18,[21] and the Convention assembled on May 20.

After the opening of the war, the requisition of troops from North Carolina, and the call for the election, Wake County citizens met in the courthouse at Raleigh to select delegates to the State convention. It was resolved that "in the opinion of the meeting," the people of Wake County were in favor of immediate secession of North Carolina and prompt ratification of the Constitution of the Confederate States of America by the Convention which was to meet on May 20. Unanimously elected were George W. Mordecai, Charles Manly, and Thomas Bragg.[22] Action in North Carolina, however, was too slow for the Confederacy, because on May 16, T. L. Clingman sent a telegram from Norfolk, Virginia, to Governor Ellis informing him that the Confederacy had passed an act admitting North Carolina to the Confederacy on her adoption of the provisional constitution of the Confederate States.[23]

When the Convention opened in the House of Commons at eleven o'clock on May 20, delegates from eighty-one counties were present. Franklin J. Moses informed the Convention that he had been appointed by the State of South Carolina "to lay before your body the ordinance whereby the said State seceded from the federal union known as the United States of America." He invited the cooperation of the Assembly "in the formation of a Southern confederacy."[24]

The action of the Convention was prompt and simple. It repealed, rescinded, and abrogated "the North Carolina ratification of the Constitution and declared North Carolina separated from the Union.

North Carolina had cooperated with the Confederacy long before it seceded, and although secession did not mean *per se* that the State would join the Confederacy, it was easier for it to do so because the Confederation government had already passed the necessary enabling legislation; therefore it did join.

Henry W. Miller of Raleigh and James T. Littlejohn of Oxford, candidates for election to the Congress from the Fourth District, announced their withdrawal from the race on April 16. Littlejohn gave as his reason for withdrawing the proclamation of President Lincoln declaring war against the South, and said that the union of the South was necessary for its salvation.[25] That this State was rendering, or was expected to render, military assistance to the Confederacy prior to May 20, is indicated by the following message from John C. McRae of Charleston, South Carolina, to Governor Ellis on April 16:

> The Gov. [sic] will furnish us Elleven [sic] Guns all mounted—one hundred pounds shot & shell for each & twenty thousand pounds of power—if at Wilmington—Hope to leave tomorrow—will require outlay to forward them— Have obtained Eight artilery [sic] May I ask your approval Answer [sic][26]

On April 19, Ellis received a message from Jefferson Davis, President of the Confederacy, at Montgomery, Alabama, in which he informed Ellis that he had ordered a distinguished engineer and two artillery officers to report to him.[27] On April 21, McRae informed Ellis from Charleston that Major Whitney of the Confederate States of America would leave that night to report to him for duty.[28] When John H.

Wheeler wrote Thomas Ruffin from Washington on March 24, he said that he had resigned his position in the federal government on March 14. He said his removal was certain and added: "It was agreed that I had discharged my duty with fidelity and ability, but a man from Ohio was hungry and asked for my place." Thomas Ruffin wrote Bartholomew Fuller advising him that in his opinion it was Fuller's duty to resign his position in Washington and return to the State as soon as possible. As soon as Ellis' reply to the request for troops was received in Washington, Fuller was determined to go home (to Fayetteville). He resigned on April 22 and left Washington on April 29.[29] The Assembly passed a resolution on May 9 authorizing Ellis to appoint a commission "to consist of one person" to represent North Carolina "at the Government of the Confederate States in Montgomery, Alabama" until the convention of the people "shall act upon the subject."[30] The original resolution provided that five be sent, but the number was subsequently reduced from five to three, and from three to one. Finally a resolution ratified on May 11 provided that if any officers have resigned "or shall hereafter resign in the army and navy of the late United States, being citizens of this State," the governor "is hereby authorized to commission said officers in the army and navy of North Carolina."[31] There were said to be *two* confederacies where one existed in the United States of America. An editorial describes them as

> a Northern Confederacy presided over by the chiefs of a party which has declared deathless hostility to the institutions of North Carolina . . . and threatens to deprive a large class of our people of that property which is secured them by our laws, [and] . . . a Southern Confederacy established upon the model of that union . . . consecrated by Washington and Jefferson . . . which guarantees to its citizens a white man's government, and secures to them justice, protection, and tranquility.[32]

Senate Bill 2 to amend Chapter LXXXVI, Section 5 of the Revised Code making it unlawful for officers of North Carolina to take the oath or affirmation to support the Constitution of the United States, was introduced in the Senate on May 2. After it was read the first time and passed, the rules were suspended and the second and third readings were made. After passing both readings, it was ordered engrossed.[33] Concrete action to alter the loyalty pattern of the people of the State was taken on June 20. On that date the Convention ratified the Constitution of the Confederate States of America and entered into federal association with the States that formed that union under the terms proposed.[34] Article IV, Section 4 of the Constitution of North Carolina, proposed and ratified in 1835, was also amended on that date "by striking out the word 'United' and inserting the word 'Confederate' before the word 'States.' "[35] Volunteers for military service were exempted from paying poll tax on June 26,[36] and jurisdiction over the forts, lighthouses, beacons, marine hospitals, and mint in North Carolina was ceded to the Confederacy on June 27.[37] The Fourth of July, 1861, was observed in some southern cities, but generally that day was allowed to pass without demonstrations. This was due to various factors, but chiefly to the actual State of war. In general, there was a diminution, if not temporary extinction of all popular interest in that day. Many people in North Carolina considered the day as an indication that the people of the State had forever severed all binding associations with the American Union. Many felt that they could not long have confidence in the people of the North and that they could never again submit to political connection with them.

The South still had a right to celebrate July 4 and to cherish the memory of "noble men like Washington," however, and as the more sane and moderate would suggest, should hold fast to her heritage.

"Let us . . . not throw away our birthright, but with the return of peace," it was suggested, "let us, as of yore, meet together on the Fourth of July, and with orations, sermons, firing of cannon, and all other popular manifestations, celebrate the birthday of Liberty."[38]

The General Assembly naturally considered itself the official law-making body of North Carolina. When it met in its second extra session on August 19, it approved some ordinances passed by the Convention by enacting legislation embodying both the text and the spirit of some of the ordinances, refused to sanction others, and enacted new legislation. In the initial meeting of the Assembly, the following resolution was introduced:

> That while we do not deem it necessary or expedient to give expression either of approval or disapproval of the general acts of the late Convention of our State, yet we do believe it proper and do hereby most heartily, cordially, sincerely, fully and entirely approve of and endorse the action thereof in severing our connection with the old, corrupt, debased, perverted and accursed Union and attaching us to the Southern Confederacy: and do assure the members of said convention, and declare to the civilized world that no act of any body politic of the State has been Received [sic] by the citizens thereof and endorsed by them with so much unanimity and enthusiasm as those [sic][39]

Many events had occurred between May 20 and August 19. The people of the State, including members of the Assembly, had experienced many of the consequences of secession. As a result the chairman of the Senate Committee on Propositions and Grievances to which this resolution was referred, reported that the Committee had considered the resolution and instructed him to report it back to the Senate. Then he asked to be discharged from any further consideration of the resolution. Thus, it was tabled on the same day it was received.

On September 19, House Bill 171 and Senate Bill 114 to amend the revised code and other laws, and providing that the words "United States" wherever they may occur in laws or parts of laws enacted thereafter be stricken out were proposed. The words "Confederate States" were to be inserted. It was read the second and third times and passed in the Senate.[40] It was ratified on September 21.[41] On the same day, the *Revised Code,* Chapter XXVI, was amended. All judges of the supreme and superior courts, all justices of the peace, and all other persons holding office in the State and required to take an oath of office before proceeding to discharge the duties of their office were required to take an oath to support the Constitution of the Confederate States of America.[42]

That the church supported union with the Confederacy is indicated by the position taken by the pro-Confederate *Church Intelligencer,* official publication of the Protestant Episcopal Church in North Carolina. "We consider the South not only as right in the present war," said the *Intelligencer,* "but as having ALL THE RIGHT on her side." It said the South had not taken a single step in the controversy "which a Christian people might not take" with a good conscience toward God and man, "and were not bound to take." The South at last "had been driven to resistance," it warned, and resistance "so slowly aroused will be terrible. . . . In the name of God, . . . let it [the war] cease, and peace be restored to our land."[43]

At a call meeting of the Concord Presbytery held at Davidson College on July 10, a resolution was adopted separating the Presbyterian Church from the General Assembly of the United States. The resolution also favored sending delegates to a convention to be held at Augusta, Georgia, in December to organize a general assembly of the Confederates.[44]

The Assembly was first to give serious consideration to the cession of land to the Confederacy, but failed largely because the Convention had not yet been called to consider the question of secession. House Bill 62 to cede to the Confederate States jurisdiction of five square miles of land in North Carolina for a seat of their government, passed the House on May 8. The next day, however, it was contended that since North Carolina was still in the Union it was unconstitutional to cede the territory of North Carolina to any other sovereignty. It would be a usurpation of power and an infringement on the rights of the people, it was argued, and the Assembly should therefore wait until the people should determine their relations with other sovereignties in the convention to be held on May 20.[45] This bill was finally tabled on May 11.[46]

On June 5, the State ceded to the Confederacy certain lands in Fayetteville which it had ceded to the United States on January 8, 1839, and all adjacent land purchased by the United States. It was to be used to erect and maintain arsenals, magazines, or other necessary buildings over the tract of land. North Carolina retained civil and criminal jurisdiction, but the Confederate government was to retain control of the land as long as it was used for the purposes expressed in the ordinance.[47] On June 11, Jefferson Davis wrote W. N. Edwards, President of the Convention of North Carolina, in his own handwriting, informing him that he had received from John W. Ellis, Governor of North Carolina, a copy of an ordinance passed by the Convention vesting in the Confederate States jurisdiction over the land. Davis said he was looking forward to the day "when in arms and everything necessary to maintain our rights, we may be independent."[48] The property in, and jurisdiction over, the forts, lighthouses, beacons, marine hospitals, a lot in Charlotte on which the mint was located, and all tracts or parcels of land previously held by the United States within North Carolina, were ceded to the Confederacy on June 27. The Confederacy was to control this property "so long as they shall severally be devoted and applied to such objects, uses, and purposes, and no longer." Civil and criminal jurisdiction were reserved to the State.[49] Thus, when we consider the more central location of North Carolina, the fact that the Confederacy was to select the territory itself, the fact that members of the Assembly were seeking desperately to cede the necessary territory—and the Convention did cede considerable territory— if North Carolina had seceded earlier, the Confederate capitol, when moved from Montgomery, might have been located in North Carolina.

As North Carolina drew closer and closer to the Confederacy it was alienated and completely isolated from the United States. In November and December, 1860, resolutions were offered in favor of both union and dissolution. This was true until North Carolina seceded in May. On December 12, the Senate attempted to amend a resolution which had been introduced on December 10 to declare the Assembly's judgment that the federal government had no right to coerce a seceding state. If South Carolina or any other State should secede, the amendment provided that federal authorities would have no power under the Constitution to make war on and subjugate the people of the States withdrawing. Meanwhile, there was an attempt to amend the amendment to provide that no state should, without consent of the Congress, "lay duty or tonnage, or keep troops or ships of war in time of peace, enter into any agreement or compact with another State or with foreign powers, or engage in any war, unless actually invaded." The idea that it was the duty of the general government "to collect peacefully if it could, but forcibly if it must, duties due it at each and every established post in these United States," was also expressed. The Senate voted 27 to 17 to postpone discussion until noon on December 13. Then

the Committee on Federal Relations was discharged from
"any further consideration of federal matters."[50] Obviously
the Committee was not discharged from further obligations
regarding federal-State questions, because on January 10,
Bedford Brown of Caswell County, member of the joint select
Committee on Federal Relations to whom was referred Senate
Resolution 17, reported the resolution as follows:

> 1. Resolved, that in the judgment of the General As-
> sembly the Federal Government has no right to coerce a
> seceding State, and South-Carolina and Florida, acting in
> their sovereign characters, through conventions, having se-
> ceded from the present Union, the federal authorities have
> now power under the Constitution to make war upon and
> subjugate these States, or any other States which hereafter
> adopt like action.
>
> 2. Resolved, that it will be the duty of the constituted
> authorities of North Carolina to resist by force the passage
> of federal troops through her territory to coerce and sub-
> jugate a seceding Southern State, and that North Carolina
> ought to resist any attempt at coercion, whether by land or
> sea, by all the means of her power.

It was ordered tabled.[51] On the next day, Samuel J. Person,
Chairman of the Committee on Foreign Relations, to which
the resolution was referred on the previous day, reported
that he had been instructed to report back and recommend
the passage of a substitute resolution which was exactly the
same as the first, except that the State of Mississippi was
added.[52] By the time the General Assembly had opened the
first extra session, it was generally conceded in North Carolina that the six seceded States could not be rightfully con-
strained by force to remain in the Union. The States in
the South were considered complete and sovereign republics
within themselves. This precluded authority vested in the
federal head to coerce by force of arms.[53] Since North Carolina had not seceded, its next problem was finding some

technic by which it could defy the government at Washington and refuse to pay tax. A resolution which was ratified on May 9 and is quoted below, helped to solve that problem.

> Whereas, Abraham Lincoln has been, and is still, endeavoring to raise money upon the faith and credit of the so-called United States Government, for the purpose of waging a wicked, unjust, unholy, and unconstitutional war upon the Southern States: and Whereas, North Carolina is neither morally or legally bound to pay or in any wise contribute to the payment of any debt incurred by the said government since the 4th day of March last: Now, therefore, to the end that there may be no misapprehension on the part of those who may invest their means in the securities of said government, it is hereby
>
> Resolved, That North Carolina ought never in any event, pay any portion of the debt or liability which may be incurred hereafter.[54]

North Carolina had supported the Confederacy from its beginning, but after the State seceded and formally joined the Confederacy in a war on the United States, it became increasingly hostile to the government at Washington.

W. Whitaker, Jr., of Raleigh wrote to N. M. Flemming, Speaker of the House, on September 19 that during April, 1861, S. Walter Scott of Raleigh was appointed "by the Lincoln government at Washington" to a route agency in North Carolina. He was to take Whitaker's place on the Raleigh and Gaston Railroad. When Whitaker heard of Scott's appointment to replace him after he had resigned, he decided that if Scott requested him to deliver the mail key "or in any way recognized said black republican government," to refuse to do so. Whitaker addressed a note to Governor Ellis to which Ellis replied:

> Your note of this date is received.
>
> The position you assume is a correct one and I approve entirely your action.

Resign your situation to nobody appointed by the 'Government' at Washington.

On the authority of this letter, Whitaker applied to the Assembly, then in session, for two month's pay for "Mr. McGowan and myself," the time which elapsed before they became the employees of the Confederate States. Since the Assembly disapproved the application, Whitaker was afraid the people would consider it unwarranted, so he decided that it was his duty to state the facts and exhibit the authority upon which his claim was based. House Resolution 231 was introduced to adjust this claim. It provided that the public treasurer be "authorized and required" to pay W. W. Whitaker and P. McGowan for their services rendered as mail agents during the months of April and May, 1861, under the direction of the Governor of the State. The resolution was promptly rejected.[55]

Correspondence addressed to Ellis in early May indicated that he had an emissary in Washington. William B. Gulich wrote him from Washington on May 2, relating what news he could. He told Ellis that he would remain there a few days longer, "probably a week or more," and could remain longer, "if you think I can be of any use to you. I have a good many republican [sic] friends, and I feel no apprehensions as to my personal safety. I shall be glad to hear from you again through the same channel of communication as before."

Gulich said he supposed there was some money in the Charlotte mint "when it was seized by you," and asked Ellis whether he would permit the fund to be drawn upon to pay debts of the United States due the citizens of North Carolina. The census takers of North Carolina had received only one half of the amount due them, he explained, and would "get no more" unless it could "be paid out of funds taken by the State." He told Ellis that if he would permit the money to be used in that way he thought he could arrange to have this class of public creditors paid.[56] On September 6, the Senate considered a resolution inquiring into charges that J. W. Thomas had reported that on a trip to New York he had in his possession Union speeches which would facilitate his movements. Also under investigation were current reports that Thomas had "purchased claims upon divers of the citizens of North Carolina" and was then "endeavoring to collect the same." This resolution was read and adopted and three senators were appointed to investigate the charges.[57] Some of the problems that developed as a result of secession in North Carolina and the struggle of the State to secure their pay as mentioned in Gulich's letter to Governor Ellis must now be considered.

A letter from James Ross Snowden, Director of the United States Mint at Philadelphia, and addressed to G. W. Caldwell, Superintendent of the Branch Mint at Charlotte, on May 13, indicated that the United States government was closing its North Carolina accounts.[58] Correspondence from John Phelan of Charlotte, dated May 6 and addressed to Ellis, meantime indicated that Phelan had been appointed United States Marshall to take the Eighth Census, and had performed his duty satisfactorily, but had been paid only two hundred fifteen dollars of the six hundred dollars due him. He urged Ellis to "lay the matter before the legislature."[59]

From the Branch Mint at Charlotte, J. H. Gibbon wrote the Governor on May 20, date of secession in North Carolina, concerning the deposits in the Charlotte Mint: "All deposits of gold received in the Mint since possession was claimed for the people of North Carolina," he said, "do not exceed five thousand dollars. This gold can not with propriety, be impressed by the ordinary devices which would prove counterfeit" and would be "objected to by the laws of the State."

His letter indicated that five-dollar coins could be minted, but "the whole number . . . would not exceed one thousand pieces." There was to be engraved on each one the declaration by Mecklenburg in 1775 and "the new declaration of 1861." There was no engrosser for the mint.

"The Director has acknowledged copies of my resignation," he said, and "a coinage for an independent state will assert an honorable distinction for North Carolina."[60]

The government of the United States had made its last payment to the men at the mint on March 31. G. W. Caldwell, Superintendent of the Mint, therefore, requested that Governor Ellis issue an order to him, in a letter addressed to Ellis on June 24, to apply as much of the mint fund as was there to payment of salaries and wages of officers and men employed during the last period, the sum of approximately $2,350.61.[61] In his report to Ellis for the year ending June 30, 1861, Caldwell indicated that he had disbursed funds belonging to the mint as follows:

For surveying the Mint Lot, to W. W. Parks, $1.50; purchase of two cords of pine wood for the engine at $4.50 each from R. S. Reid, $9.00; payment of $75.00 to A. P. Gray for watching the Mint for three months at $25.00 a month; and payment to others for watching the Mint, viz "Gray, $50.00 for five of his servants."[62]

The salaries of the mint officers at Charlotte were as follows: G. W. Caldwell, Superintendent, $500.00; John H. Gibbon, $375.00; Emmor Graham, $375.00; and William F. Strange, $250.00.[63]

Other problems arose when the United States Post Office closed its accounts in North Carolina and the transition from the United States postal service to the Confederate States postal service was made. During the interval before the Confederate service was organized, the States attempted to assume the responsibility of providing mail service. H. P. White of Merry Mount wrote Governor Ellis on May 1 as follows:

I address you a few hasty lines to know if I am exempted from Military duty being Post Master—I am Willing to serve as the Most of Men but being surrounded by distressing circumstances I do not Want to Leave home—I am willing to serve as home guard—& the circumstances is This my wife died the 23d day of March last & left me with three little children—1-7 months—1-2 years & the other one about 1, years [sic] old I have a small farm with 9 servants Dwelling House Meet House corn crib &c I shall have to leave in the care of servants store House goods bond, & accounts and no one to attend to them . . .—sir it is true that many would render an excuse to stay at home—but take the above circumstances to yourself and you or any other but what Man would [not] desire to stay with there motherless children & defend them against anything that might occur at home sir you will confer a kind favor upon me by an answer to the above Reference.[64]

A. Dixon, postmaster at Elevation in Johnston County, wrote Ellis on May 7 that "I see in the Standard May 1st where it says that the mail carriers will be paid by the State, &c dear sir I desire some Instruction [sic] as Postmaster." Dixon wanted to know to whom he was to send his monthly registers, "to who shall I make quarterly return to, [sic] in what way should the Postage be paid, and what shall I do with the stamps I have received from the Government on hand." He said he was charged with the stamps and did not wish to "lay myself liable in this distracted condition of the country."[65]

The answer to some of these questions was contained in legislation enacted by the General Assembly. Senate Resolution 82, introduced in the May and June session of the Assembly, provided that if mail service should be discontinued, the governor would take over the service of the post office. Postage rates were to be the same, and the governor was to draw on the public treasury for the necessary operating funds. This resolution was recommended by the Committee, passed the first, second, and third readings, and was ordered engrossed.[66] A similar resolution was ratified on May 11. It provided that if the mail service of North Carolina should be discontinued, the governor was authorized and empowered to take charge of the post offices and continue mail service on the routes then in operation as he believed the public interest required. The governor's administration of this service was to continue "until such time as provision shall be made for their operation." He was authorized to collect postage at the rate then charged and to draw on the public treasurer "for such sums of money as may be necessary to defray the expenses" over and above the receipts from postage.[67] On May 13, 1861, Postmaster General John J. Reagen of the Confederacy announced that his department was well enough organized to take over the service. He issued a proclamation directing that on the close of business on May 31, 1861, each postmaster should render his account and money to the United States and forward to the Post Office Department, Washington, D. C., the accounts and money due. Montgomery Blair, United States Postmaster General, suspended postal service to the states of the Confederacy on June 1, 1861.

Chapter Eight

Mobilization for Defense

S ECTIONALISM became increasingly worse after repeal of the Missouri Compromise and organization of the Republican party four years prior to the 1860 election. The resulting tensions led to a moderate but general mobilization more than six months prior to either of the 1860 national conventions. This mobilization was quickened by the nomination of Abraham Lincoln as the Republican candidate for president.

By January 1, the citizens of Mecklenburg County seemed thoroughly aroused on the military question and had organized three cavalry companies. The *Asheville Citizen* referred to the Charlotte area as "the hornet nest region" and said it was "preparing to sting when the time comes." All who could "possibly make it convenient," particularly "property holders and slaveholders," were urged to encourage military organization by their membership in one of these companies. Those unable to muster were asked to contribute liberally to purchase uniforms for those who were unable to equip themselves. Volunteers with horses could "be accomodated under Captain Harrison and those who have none" could "take it afoot under Capt [*sic*] Bryce or Captain Owens." Ministers, physicians, and attorneys were enrolling for duty.[1] Having spent one million dollars for locomotives made in the North during 1859, southern railroads at the beginning of 1860 were planning to initiate a combined movement for a southern supply of equipment and materials.[2] A meeting was called in Asheville in mid-January, 1860, to urge ladies "to take an active part in the movement now so general, the encouragement of Southern enterprise." On June 12 of that year, citizens of Buncombe County met in the courthouse to consider the feasibility of manufacturing various kinds of goods in the South.[3] Having developed before the 1860 election, "patronize the South" advertisements were prevalent long before the Civil War.[4] Meanwhile, as if hedging himself against "any eventuality," Willie Reddick of Gates County sold "to a Southern planter 85 Negroes for $85,000." Payment was to be made in six annual installments, with interest. Made on October 5, this was the largest sale of slaves "ever known in our section," and included "young and old, his entire family, save six."[5]

By mid-January, 1861, the wild struggle to achieve self-sufficiency had led to the seizure of Fort Caswell. Josiah Turner of Orange County introduced a resolution in the Senate on January 7, requesting Governor John W. Ellis to inform the Senate whether "any portion of the citizens of North Carolina had consulted him upon the propriety of taking possession of the forts of the United States in North Carolina." If so, the resolution requested the names of the citizens and information as to their proposals. It was also resolved that the governor inform the Senate whether he had been advised of any plan by which the forts were to be occupied on or before March 4 "by any authority or force other than that of the United States." The Senate voted 24 to 12 that the resolution be tabled.[6] Asserting a moderating influence in this crisis was a Senate resolution introduced on January 12. It expressed regret and profound astonishment that military companies composed of North Carolina citizens had seized Fort Caswell, "one of the Forts of the United States at the mouth of the Cape Fear River," and requested that Ellis provide certain specific information regarding this operation. The resolution requested that the governor provide the Senate information as to whether he had been "consulted and advised on the subject." If so, the Senate was to be informed by whom and given their places of residence. The Senate voted 25 to 17 to table the question.[7] A second resolution introduced on that date provided, first, that the General Assembly appeal to President Buchanan to withdraw the troops from the Atlantic and Gulf States and use his influence to favor suspension of the revenue laws as far as they apply to States which have declared or may declare themselves out of the Union. The purpose of this was to prevent conflict between the State and federal government and to allow time for an honorable and peaceful adjustment of the difficulties between the North and the South. The second provision was that the Assembly appeal to the States out of the Union to exercise in a spirit of conciliation "all the forebearance consistent with the honor and safety to prevent conflict between themselves and the General Government." The governor was to forward copies of the resolution of President Buchanan and the governors of the States out of the Union.[8] Some of the official correspondence concerning the first seizure of the forts seem to indicate that military and State officials were also conciliatory, but information as to who captured the forts was contradictory.

On January 11, Governor Ellis addressed an order to Graham Davis, private secretary and acting adjutant-general, and Colonel John L. Cantwell, who was commanding the 30th Regiment of the North Carolina Marines during the illness of the commander. Ellis said that he had been informed unofficially that Captain S. D. Thurston of the Smithville Guards had, with his company, taken possession of Fort Caswell and was holding it. The informant assured Ellis that Thurston was a gallant officer and was actuated by patriotic motives as a citizen of North Carolina, which Ellis said he did not doubt. Because of relations existing between the United States government and this State, however, the governor could find no legal authority for occupation of the United States forts located in North Carolina. Unable to sustain Thurston's "patriotic motives," he said he was compelled to order Caswell restored to the possession of authorities of the United States government, specifically ordering Colonel Cantwell to

> proceed to Smithville, upon receipt of this communication and communicate orders to captain Thurston to withdraw his troops from Fort Caswell.

> You will also investigate and report the facts of the transaction to this department.[9]

Cantwell wrote Ellis on January 16 from his headquarters in Wilmington, enclosing a copy of his order which had been issued in conformity with the governor's instructions, and the reply of Major J. J. Hendrick to this order. He told Ellis that from the information he had received, it seemed that Fort Caswell was occupied by citizens of the State as a consequence of a report that federal troops had been ordered to that point. The United States sergeant in charge there remained in the fort but was under no restraint. "Captain Thurston desires to state," he concluded, "that his company, the Smithville Guards, did not occupy the Fort" and that he believes these to be the facts in the case.[10] Cantwell, meanwhile, had written Major Hendrick on January 12 that in obedience to the order of Governor Ellis, it was his duty to direct Hendrick to "withdraw the troops" under his command from Fort Caswell and "restore the fort to the custody of the officer of the United States whom you found in charge."[11] "I have to inform you," wrote Hendrick on January 13, "that we, as North-Carolinians, will obey his command. This post will be evacuated to-morrow [sic] at 9 o'clock, A.M."[12]

Ellis reported to James Buchanan, President of the United States, on January 12 that reliable information had reached

Raleigh that on January 8, Forts Johnson and Caswell were seized by State troops and "persons resident" in that vicinity "in an irregular manner." He said he immediately issued military orders requiring that they be restored, "which order will be executed this day."

This popular uprising, he said, was caused by a report that it was the purpose of the national administration to coerce the Southern States and that troops were on the way to garrison the southern ports and to begin the work of subjugation. Ellis concluded

> I would most earnestly appeal to your excellency to strengthen my hands in my efforts to preserve the public order here, by placing it in my power to give public assurance that no measures of force are contemplated towards us. . . .
>
> Should I receive assurance that no troops will be sent to this State prior of the 4th of March next . . . all will be peace and quiet here, and the property of the United States will be fully protected as heretofore. If, however, I am unable to get such assurances I will not undertake to answer for the consequences.

Ellis submitted copies of the correspondence with the government at Washington, but did not mention Fort Macon because, he said, he "had not heard that it had been in any way interfered with by our citizens."[13]

A letter from J. Holt, Secretary of War ad interim to Ellis, dated January 15, acknowledged the letter to the President. Holt said he was directed to say that the North Carolina forts, "in common with all other forts, arsenals, and public property of the United States, are in charge of the President," and that if assailed, no matter from what quarter or under what pretext, it was his duty to protect them "by all the means which the law has placed at his disposal." It was not the President's intention to garrison the forts at any time, he said, because "he considers them entirely safe" under the shelter of "that law-abiding sentiment for which the people of North Carolina have been distinguished." If they should be attacked or menaced with danger of being seized and taken from the United States, however, the President could not escape his constitutional obligation to defend and preserve them.[14]

Holt expressed gratitude at the promptness with which Ellis ordered expulsion of the lawless men who occupied Forts Johnson and Caswell. That action, he said, he regarded as in complete harmony with "the honor and patriotic character of the people of North Carolina whom you so worthily represent." The "very satisfactory and patriotic assurances given by your excellency" justified Holt, he concluded, "in entertaining the confident expectation" that no contingency would arise which would make it necessary to use force to defend the forts.[15] The House of Commons requested that it be informed of the correspondence in a resolution dated January 17, which reads as follows:

> Resolved that his Excellency the Governor be requested to inform this House whether he has any correspondence with the President of the United States, or any other officer of the State or Federal government relative to the occupation of Forts Caswell and Macon or either of them by the militia of this State, or any body of armed citizens; or as to any intention of the Government to place troops in said forts: and if so, to communicate such correspondence to the House of Commons.[16]

A Senate resolution dated January 14 condemned the action of the "certain citizens of North Carolina who seized Fort Caswell."[17] The official attitude throughout the entire crisis was a conciliatory one.

In the second seizure of the forts in mid-April, the general attitude was less conciliatory. Governor Ellis received a telegram from S. I. Person at Wilmington on April 15 requesting instructions. "Our people will take the Forts—Send us your orders," he said, "or we go without them and hold against all powers."[18] On April 18, Ellis received a telegram from F. L. Clingman at Charleston to "take at once the Fayetteville arsenal" and to aid Governor Fletcher in "taking Norfolk."[19] On that same day, Ellis received a second telegram from Charleston advising him to "detach twelve men of an artillery company to proceed here to be drilled in the management of Columbiad." He said they would become familiarized with the work by the time the guns were ready.[20] North Carolina was still in the Union, but by early May this increasing belligerency was expressed in many ways. Old enough to recall the troubles of the War of 1812, one woman of Church and Union Hills ordered her three sons to shoulder their muskets in defense of the State, or never again claim to be her children. Another woman with grandchildren offered to accompany the First Regiment as a nurse.[21] On May 8, House Resolution 8, thanking Governor Ellis for taking possession of the forts and arsenals which belonged to the federal government and "patriotic motives which led to their capture," was read, passed and adopted.[22] In calling out the troops and in his efforts "to put the State in a posture of defense," the resolution reads, the governor "rendered important service for which our thanks are due and heartily tendered."[23]

Tangible support of this belligerency was expressed in January when legislation was ratified appropriating three hundred thousand dollars to purchase arms and munitions of war. Major D. H. Hill of Charlotte and Colonel C. C. Tew of Hillsboro were to "constitute a military commission" to "advise the Governor in the manner of providing the State with arms and munitions."

In a telegram to Governor Ellis from Charlotte on April 18, Hill informed Ellis that a Captain Ramseur, a graduate of West Point and an artillery officer in Charlotte, was anxious to serve Ellis and asked Ellis whether he could "send him to the forts." On that same day he received a telegram from F. W. Pickins of Charlotte in response to a telegram that Ellis had sent him. Pickins said he rejoiced "to hear that your Noble State is moving." He said that McRae had received from him on that day "eleven cannon of large caliber," shot, twenty thousand pounds of powder, and other items for the forts, and concluded: "You have my heart and hand—Let me hear often." Horace Mayfield wrote Ellis from Weldon on April 22 that "we hereby tender to you our services as cavalry troops of the County of Warren to be included in the ten thousand volunteers."[24]

A resolution passed on May 1 and ratified three days later provided that any portion of the three hundred thousand dollars which remain unexpended be placed at the disposal of the governor to be expended at his discretion "in arming, organizing, equipping, provisioning, and transporting troops" by that time raised in the State "for the defense of the South."[25] On May 10, the governor was authorized to employ militia, military, and naval forces of the State and to call for twenty thousand and twelve-month volunteers. Their pay and allowance were to be the same as that of the soldiers in the army of the Confederate States of America.[26] Ellis was also authorized on that date to provide for the provisioning, while passing through the State, of such troops from the Southern States as might travel through North Carolina on their way to Virginia. The necessary expenses were to be paid out of any money in the treasury.[27] A resolution ratified on May 11 provided that if any officers had resigned or should thereafter resign their commissions "in the army and navy of the late United States," being citizens of this State, the governor was thereby authorized to commission said officers in the army and navy of North Carolina. Any such officers so commissioned would receive the same rank and pay as officers of similar rank in the service of the Confederate States of America.[28] Thus, by the time North Carolina seceded on May 20, it had not only established friendly relations with the Confederacy but had made some provision for defense and was cooperating fully with the Confederate armies.

Troops from North Carolina were authorized to join the Confederate States on August 30. The commanders were to report to the governor the number and type of his forces before leaving the State, but the companies, regiments, legions, and other organizations had the right to select their officers, "if consistent with the laws of the Confederate States of America." To enable the State to meet this obligation, the treasury was authorized to issue one million dollars in treasury notes, redeemable on January 1, 1867, in legislation ratified on September 20, 1861.[29]

A majority of the justices of any county being present, they could still elect to lay and collect a school tax under provisions of an act passed on September 21, but the basic clause in this school law was superseded. Chapter LXVI, Section 32 of the revised code which required courts to lay and collect tax for common schools was repealed.[30] Defense spending had greatly increased by the end of the year, so on December 1, the treasury was authorized to issue notes not exceeding three million dollars at any time before January 1, 1863.[31]

Throughout the latter half of 1861, companies of volunteers were constantly being organized. Ed. Graham Haywood and W. R. Cox announced on June 12 that they were "raising a company of infantry . . . for the service of the war against Abraham Lincoln." They were receiving men for only one year at a time and paying a ten-dollar bounty when they were mustered into the service. They were to be paid eleven dollars a month and provided food and clothing during the time they were in the service. The entrance to their recruiting office was on Hargett Street in the rear of Williams and Haywood Drug Store in Raleigh.[32] An act was ratified on September 7 providing arms for an independent

North Carolina regiment organized by Wharton J. Green of
Warren County and Marcus Erwin of Buncombe County
and tendered to the Confederate States. Since difficulty had
arisen in providing the regiment with arms, an order of
Governor Clark and one from Colonel J. A. Bradford, Chief
of Ordinance, permitted Green "to draw upon the public
treasurer" from time to time money necessary to purchase
arms and equipment "not to exceed $50,000," provided he
gave security approved by the treasurer.[33] A volunteer company commanded by James G. Burr was incorporated as the
Independent Guards by legislative action on September 11.
All of its members were exempted from county or superior
court jury service while active members of the company.[34]
Clark was authorized on September 12 to receive a company
of cavalry volunteers then "being raised in North Carolina
by R. S. Tucker, Wiley G. Riddick, Will M. Boylan, Fabius
Perry, J. Robert Jeffreys, T. J. Utley, J. B. G. Grimes, *et al.*
for 12 months." This company was to furnish its own horses,
arms, and equipment and receive compensation for their
horses at the rate of forty cents a day while in service. They
were to receive the same pay and allowances, rations, and for-
age as provided other cavalry companies in service in the
Confederate States. This company had the right to elect its
own officers who were to be commissioned by and under
direction of the governor and assigned such duties as the
State might require or attached to any regiment or regiments
of North Carolina troops in or out of the State.[35] On September 23, Clark was authorized to receive another company of
cavalry raised by Alexander Murchison on the same terms.[36]
Governor Clark was authorized on September 20 to establish
a military camp "for the purpose of raising, drilling, and
equipping troops at the North Fork of New River, near the
Tennessee line."[37] Senate Resolution 25, introduced in the
Senate on August 22, provided that the members of the
second extra session of the General Assembly be organized

into two companies of infantry or cavalry, with the privilege of electing their own officers; but it was tabled on the following day.

By mid-August, Edward Cantwell, Clerk of the House of Commons, had assumed duty as an officer of the volunteers serving in Virginia. On August 16, he tendered his resignation to the Honorable William J. Dortch, Speaker of the House. The House accepted his resignation immediately and Dortch sent a message to the Speaker of the Senate reporting Cantwell's resignation, its acceptance by the House, and selection of James H. Moore to fill that vacancy.

As early as May 6, a bill was introduced and read, passing the first reading in the Senate, providing for enlistment of free men of color between the ages of sixteen and sixty in the state militia, but it was tabled. A bill authorizing the governor to muster the Cherokee Indians into the service of the State was taken up for the first time on September 9. It passed the third reading in the Senate on September 19 and was engrossed. House Bill 203, Senate Bill 143, to authorize officers to impress certain persons into the service of their companies, originated in the House on the same day as the Cherokee Indian muster bill. It provided that all captains and commissioned officers of companies of State troops and volunteers for twelve months or less "be authorized to impress into service . . . as servants to perform the necessary labors of the camps—free male persons of color between the ages of eighteen and fifty." All persons impressed or who thereafter volunteered, were to be paid six dollars a month at the same time the members of the company were paid. This atrocious bill reached the Senate on September 14 and was tabled on September 20. Slaves could be, and were soon thereafter, impressed into service, because an undated resolution found among the legislative papers for the 1861-62 session of the Assembly indicates that one slave had died from exposure and disease while working on the fortifications near Kinston. Resolution 95, prepared or acted upon about December 8, 1861, provided that the public treasurer pay to Pherbie Johnson twenty-five hundred dollars "for a negro man Campbell, who died in consequence of exposure and disease contracted while at work on the fortifications near Kinston in this State." No record as to whether this bill was presented or of action on it could be found.

"We are in the midst of war and revolution. North Carolina would have stood by the Union," Jonathan Worth wrote on May 30, "but for the conduct of the national administration which for folly and simplicity exceeds anything in modern history, as North Carolina is strictly a unit for resistance and everywhere is heard the sound of drum and fife. Shubal is drilling his company. Several other companies are nearly formed in this county. . . . I feel that we can not be conquered." On September 30, he reported that "two new companies from Randolph are about ready to go into camp." On December 7, he concluded:

This State is a unit against the Lincoln Government. It is one great military camp. Some ten thousand troops are in the field. The old Union men are as determined as the original secessionists. The State is totally alienated from the Lincoln Government and will fight to extermination before they will reunite with the North.[38]

That these troops expected the maximum freedom consistent with order and discipline is indicated by a resolution in regard to the inspection of troops ratified on September 21. It provided that in mustering volunteers into service in North Carolina for twelve months or for the duration of the war, it would not be lawful to order such volunteers to be stripped of their clothing to be examined. Examination by the surgeon was to be made only upon inspection of the men in line, and such private inquiry and examination, without undressing, or "as the surgeon shall think such volunteer may require." However, the surgeon reserved the power to examine a particular defect, disease, or injury which would render the volunteer unfit for service.[39]

With the States of the lower South and Texas already blockaded, seizure of United States property, obstruction of revenue collections, and arrest and detainment of federal officials as prisoners without due legal process by persons who said they were acting under Virginia and North Carolina authorities led to the blockading of the ports of North Carolina and Virginia in a proclamation issued on April 27.[40] On May 3, still more than two weeks prior to the secession of North Carolina, a garrison of twenty-two hundred men marched on the Fayetteville arsenal. With the arsenal surrounded without force, the armament thus secured helped make it possible for the State to engage in the Civil War either to preserve its liberties on its own soil, or to assist any of the Confederate States which needed assistance. To some persons in the State, it was then obvious that the battle could be decided in the District of Columbia. There was "no doubt" that North Carolina forts were prepared "to resist any attack upon them by the Black Republicans and company after company should be sent from here to aid in the capture of Washington." With "what was once the National Capitol in their hands," the Confederate States were expected soon to be recognized as a sovereign and independent nation.[41] Ellis was authorized to erect batteries or other fortifications at, or near, the inlets of Hatteras, Ocracoke, and other places on the coast or rivers, as in his judgment the public safety might demand. Under provisions of this authority which was granted on May 11, he could purchase or charter and equip such steamers or other vessels as might be necessary for defense of the seacoast of the State. Then he could draw upon the treasury for the necessary money.[42]

In the case of both the Union and the Confederacy, we know that the Civil War was perhaps the most poorly organized and mal-administered of all of the wars in our history. Even in the North, the States carried on activities and assumed responsibilities that not only would be considered federal functions, but would now be regarded as endangering the sovereignty of the United States. We also know that the innumerable activities carried on in North Carolina were poorly organized and poorly coordinated.

"I fully agree with you," Kenneth Rayner wrote Judge Thomas Ruffin on July 18, "that our militia system should be thoroughly reorganized, and brought to some efficiency so as to be made effectual in case of necessity." With regard to the proposed selective service plan which would permit drafting for military purposes "all . . . able-bodied men between eighteen and forty-five," Rayner suggested that "unless in case of actual invasion, I doubt the propriety of it." He said this law would leave the county in too defenseless a condition and disorganize and derange "all . . . the industrial pursuits of our laboring white population." He was afraid it would be misunderstood in the North and "enspirit our enemies with the idea that our people are not willing to volunteer . . . that we have to resort to compulsion to get our men in the fields."[43]

J. E. Martin, Adjutant-General of State Troops, sought specific information on the troops on July 23 by addressing correspondence to the captains of all companies of twelve-month volunteers accepted by the governor but not assigned to regiments. These commanders were directed to report immediately by letter to Martin's office the strength and amount of arms, "if any," in each company. Other companies that had been formed but not theretofore accepted by the governor were also requested to report.[44] The information provided in these reports was useful, because the constituents were demanding that their kin in the service be paid. W. T. Dortch, Secretary of the House, wrote Governor Clark on August 19, informing him of the following resolution which had passed the House:

That the Governor be required to inform the House whether any arrangement has been made to pay the North Carolina troops and volunteers and whether payment is to be
made by the State or Confederate government.[45]

Clark replied by sending the Speaker of the House a special
report of the quartermaster and paymaster general on August 21.[46] The report was signed by Colonel L. O. B. Branch
who also inclosed a letter from A. C. Myers, Quartermaster
General, dated July 5. Volunteers were paid by the Confederate States from the date of their muster into the service,
the letter explained, but after the transfer of the muster
rolls to the Confederate service. Those with no prior service
then were paid from the date of the order directing them
to proceed to any destination by the War Department.[47]
There was still some dissatisfaction among the people of
North Carolina as attested by the following resolution, ratified on September 13:

Resolved, that the Governor be authorized and required to
appoint two commissioners . . . to proceed to the City of
Richmond and confer with authorities of the Confederate
States Government in relation to the defense of the seacoast
of North Carolina, and the enlistment, equipment, subsistence, and pay of the troops of this State, and that they
report results of their conference to the General Assembly
or to the Governor.[48]

Clark appointed George Davis and L. O. B. Branch to go to
Richmond to consult the President and Confederate authorities regarding North Carolina coast defenses and provision
for winter clothing for the troops. In their report these men
said that it was decided that the troops would have to be
provided for by the States from which they volunteered.[49]

Most of the funds appropriated for military and general
war needs were provided in the first and second extra sessions of the Assembly after North Carolina had left the
Union. Legislation ratified early in the first extra session pro-

vided that the treasury was authorized as early as was practical
to issue treasury notes amounting to $500,000. The treasurer
was authorized to borrow an additional $1,000,000 from the
banks of North Carolina at 6 per cent interest. If $1,500,000
was not sufficient to meet the demands of the public treasury
"during the next two years," the treasurer was authorized to
issue treasury notes "on the faith and credit of the State"
to the amount of $1,000,000. If the $2,500,000 was not sufficient to meet the demands during the aforesaid period,
the treasurer was authorized to borrow an additional
$500,000. Another $500,000 was authorized if the resulting
$3,000,000 was insufficient, and an additional $750,000 could
likewise be collected through the sale of notes if the $3,500,-
000 was not sufficient. Section 7 of the law authorized the
treasurer to borrow money not exceeding $5,000,000. Banks
were not required to resume specie payments while any
amount of the loan authorized remained unpaid.[50]

On June 28, up to $3,200,000 was appropriated to meet
demands of the public treasury for the two ensuing years.
It was to be raised by issuing ten-, twenty-five-, and fifty-cent
notes amounting to $200,000 and by borrowing $3,000,000
from banks by issuing State bonds.[51] The treasurer was authorized to issue $800,000 in treasury notes "to provide for
the defense of the State" on September 18,[52] and on September 20, he was authorized to issue $1,000,000 in treasury
notes.[53]

After Confederate officials ruled on August 21 that North
Carolina and the other Southern States in the Confederacy
would have to pay their own troops, the Assembly took
concrete action to compensate its volunteers. An act to
authorize the governor "to pay the officers and privates of
the First Regiment of volunteers one month's pay" was
ratified on August 27.[54] However, on September 13 when
the governor was "authorized and required to instruct the
paymaster" to pay all of the North Carolina soldiers and offi-

cers in the State, and regiments and companies in Virginia, if not paid by the Confederate States, he was required to "immediately thereafter make a requisition upon the proper authorities of the Confederacy for refunding the money." The power and authority was also extended to the governor to pay any regiments or battalions then being formed under the authority of the State.[55]

A bill was introduced in the Senate on September 7 which would have raised the salary of non-commissioned officers in the State and federal service to fifteen dollars. The Senate Committee on Military Affairs recommended that it not pass and it was tabled on September 19.[56]

The volunteers sometimes soon deserted their company, as indicated by an announcement by Peter Mallett, Captain of Company C, Third Regiment, of the North Carolina State Troopers. On July 30, Captain Mallett offered to pay a thirty-dollar reward "for the apprehension and delivery of deserter Burwell W. Hodges at any jail or Military Post in the State." Mallett said Hodges was residing in Harnett County about ten miles from Averasboro, had hazel eyes, black hair, and a dark complexion and was five feet, ten inches tall. He had enlisted on May 20 at the age of twenty and deserted on June 10. This announcement was also in a newspaper on September 19.[57]

Various economic measures, both voluntary and compulsory, were also taken to promote the war. A bill "to exempt sewing machines from execution" was introduced in the Senate on the opening day of the first extra session of the Assembly. With a provision that all machines used by women or mechanics should be exempted from seizure under execution, it passed the Senate, but no record of further action could be found.[58] By that time the women of Raleigh had formed a society to contribute to the defense of the State. They made, and "turned over to the adjutant-general for the troops," fifteen hundred mattresses, six hundred towels, three thousand uniform jackets, two hundred pantaloons, four hundred fatigue shirts, and two hundred haversacks during the week ending Thursday or Friday, May 9 or 10. Making use of the basement of "the new Baptist church," the offices of the governor and his private secretary in the capital, and the hall of the House of Commons to carry on these activities, they were assisted by "several free colored women" who voluntarily "tendered their services."[59] In an announcement "to the ladies" on July 29, Cumberland County residents who were "still willing to do something for their country" were reminded that they could "find a blouse for each member of the Cumberland Cavalry to make up at the store of Mr. Alex. Johnson, Jr., this afternoon at 4:00 or tomorrow." Those who could not go there to secure the materials could send their names and they would be sent to them.[60] Persons who wished to sign contracts to make clothing for the Army of North Carolina could get terms and goods enough to clothe one company to be made up in their own neighborhoods. Parties could also furnish the cloth which would be paid for by the State.[61]

Various exemptions and other considerations were given soldiers and their families. House Bill 30 to exempt military personnel from arrest under civil process was approved by the House with minor amendments and sent to the Senate on May 10.[62] Poll tax payment was required in 1861, but persons who had volunteered for service prior to August 15 were exempted.[63] W. H. Wyatt, a druggist, announced on August 1 that families of volunteers from Salisbury who were ill and endorsed by their physicians as unable to pay for drugs would be given free medicine.[64] The Soldiers' Aid Society of Raleigh accepted voluntary contributions for soldiers[65] and the Rowan County Soldiers' Aid Society, headed by Mrs. D. A. Davis, announced that it would receive clothing, fruit, nuts, and food for the soldiers of that county.[66]

Merchants unable to buy on credit advertised that they were adopting the cash system.[67] Kenneth Rayner returned $45.40, his pay and allowance as a member of the Convention during May, 1861. In his letter, dated August 21, he said he wished the sum tendered to be appropriated "to the fund pledged to be raised by the authorities of the county for the support of the families of the volunteers from Hertford County."[68] The governor's proclamation prohibiting exportation beyond State lines of bacon, leather, and shoes, "except by or through the orders of proper officers and agents of the Confederate States," was approved by the House of Commons on September 21. House Resolution 281 which favored the governor's proclamation would have also authorized Governor Clark to extend his order to include "all woolen goods and goods made in part of wool," but it was tabled in the Senate.[69] Clark issued another proclamation on November 25, however, prohibiting exportation of bacon, pork beef, leather, men's shoes, woolen goods, jeans, linseys, and blankets, "except through orders of proper officials of the Confederate Government."[70]

Just as the tariff of 1789, the Continental System, the Orders in Council, and the Embargo of 1807 encouraged early American manufacturing, so the conflict between the Union and certain southern States and the resulting blockade and isolation of all but the border States of the South promoted the development of industry in North Carolina. A clear indication of developing sectional prejudices is indicated in the following announcement which was made continuously from November 21, 1860, to June, 1861:

TO THE PUBLIC

THE SUBSCRIBER, in consequence of unwarrantable reports having been put in circulation to the effect that the Piano Manufactory for which he is Agent is a Black Republican concern, located in Massachusetts, begs leave to advertise his friends and the public that he is not now and never has been, acting as Agent for such establishment.

The Pianos he offers for sale are manufactured by a southern gentleman in a southern State.

Mr. HENRY GAEHLE of Baltimore, is the manufacturer, and his Pianos are warranted. Those who prefer to patronize Southern manufactures instead of Northern or Black Republican ones can be supplied by

CHAS. O. PAPE, Agt.

Charlotte, N. C.[71]

A. C. McKethan's announcement was made continuously from December 17, 1860, to June 10, 1861. He constantly informed his friends "in North Carolina and throughout the South who wish to encourage Southern industry" that he had available and was "daily finishing" a large assortment of vehicles of every description "faithfully made by experienced workmen in each branch." He said that "orders from the South" would "receive prompt attention."

The *Wilmington Journal* looked upon the efforts of Weill and Anathan to begin on an extensive scale the manufacture of cheap clothing in Wilmington as "a move in the right direction." "It is so much toward real independence," the *Journal* said on June 10, "and besides it will supply a means of earning a living to hundreds of worthy men and girls who are only anxious for an opportunity to do so."[72] J. C. Carpenter, agent for the Kinston Shoe Factory, announced continuously from June 24, 1860, to mid-June, 1861, that this factory was in successful operation and was soliciting orders for "negro [*sic*] Brogans and Boots."[73] William Carter, S. S. Carter, David A. Carter, and John Q. Carter of Carterville in Chatham County, trading as William Carter and Sons, announced from October 25, 1860, to January 21, 1861, that they were the only manufacturers in the state producing "a number one article of KIP SHOES and Negro BROGANS, without welts."[74]

The Assembly took concrete action on December 18, 1860, when the House Military Affairs Committee introduced a resolution that the governor be requested "to furnish to this House" such information as he had and could procure in the next thirty days as to the probable cost of establishing a foundry for casting cannon and the establishment of a manufactory of arms of all kinds. The House concurred, and Governor Ellis transmitted the available information on January 10. He estimated that an armory capable of manufacturing five thousand muskets a year would cost forty-eight thousand dollars and noted that, for an additional ten thousand dollars, production capacity could be raised to fifteen thousand rifle muskets a year.

"We would agree to satisfy you," Ellis said, "that we have the highest talent and experience in making guns . . . to be found in any country, our engineer having gotten up the Enfield Armory and superintended it for five years, which is, perhaps, the first in the world."

The necessary gun-making machinery, for five-thousand-gun capacity, complete and erected for use, would cost $176,000. The required staff officers were a superintendent and a master armorer at a salary of $3,000, three foremen at $1,000 dollars each, two inspectors at $2,000, and a master mechanic at $1,500 a year. The cost of completing each gun was estimated to be $13.60. A separate estimate of the cost of construction of a cannon foundry was $75,000 to $100,000.[76] The need for ammunition remained acute. On April 26, the *Western Sentinel* reported that the time for "wasting our ammunition in firing statutes is past. The South needs all her powder for sterner work. North Carolina especially is possessed of none too much. We may have enough, but we have none to burn uselessly." In firing a few dozen rounds from "the old gun," the *Sentinel* warned, the State could waste more powder that would be necessary to annihilate a Union regiment.[77] The Assembly began action on the various proposals on May 7. On that day, House Bill 22 to provide for the manufacture of arms and ammunition of war was passed in the House and passed in the Senate with amendments. Senate Bill 64, to encourage the manufacture of gun powder in Mecklenburg County, and various other bills were introduced in the Assembly,[78] but no such legislation was ratified until September 4. In order to encourage the manufacture of gun powder, the governor was authorized on that date to subscribe stock or loan money to any company for making powder, or building of any powder factory, and to buy machinery to make power. Not more than four such companies could be formed, however, and not more then ten thousand dollars could be advanced to any one factory or mill.[79] The governor was specifically authorized to draw from the treasury and loan to the North Carolina Powder Manufacturing Company in Mecklenburg County the sum of ten thousand dollars.[80]

Almost as indispensable in winning the war was a commodity known as salt. When the *Nashville Union* noticed that this commodity had "materially advanced in the market," it declared the advance due to fear that the stock in the Southern States would be exhausted before a supply could be obained, a direct consequence of the blockade. There was a firm in Smythe County, Virginia, manufacturing large quantities annually, and there were believed to be other places in the South where it might be manufactured. The Union, nonetheless, advised that "it would be well for enterprising capitalists to turn their attention to the subject."[81] The *Wilmington Journal* wrote on January 10:

> Salt.—Make Salt; you can do so all around the coast by evaporating the sea water. This is the way it is made in Turks Island. If the blockade is really made effective, we must make Salt. We must make Salt to cure beef, pork, and so forth. Salt is now too high. It is much higher than it ought to be.[82]

Official attention was finally given to this salt problem on December 6, when the Convention ratified "an Ordinance in Regard to the Salt Supply." The ordinance authorized appointment by the Convention of a commissioner to manufacture salt for the use of the people and to furnish it to the people of each county "at the most convenient depot on the railroad to such county, or some navigable waters." The consumer was to pay the cost of manufacturing and transportation at the time of delivery. One hundred thousand dollars was appropriated for that purpose. The ordinance was to continue in effect "during the continuance of the present war, unless the Legislature shall otherwise order." The Salt Commissioner was to be paid fifteen hundred dollars annually and his traveling expenses.[83]

As the Civil War approached, four distinct groups were perceptible in North Carolina. To the extreme right and the extreme left were the ardent pro-slavery, pro-southern, and pro-secessionist faction, and the ardent pro-Unionist. In the center was the more moderate pro-slavery and pro-southern faction, which loved North Carolina and the South but which was nonetheless anti-secessionist. There was a fourth faction composed of neutrals.

Between the spring of 1860 and spring, 1861, there was a constant shifting of loyalties. The pro-slavery, pro-southern, and pro-secessionist faction increased in size and strength as the other factions declined. After North Carolina seceded, the pro-slavery, pro-southern, anti-secessionist faction, the pro-Unionists, and the neutrals were compelled to rush to the incipient Confederate frontier and join in the struggle to protect their interests. Thus did all of North Carolina mobilize for defense.

Notes

NOTES TO CHAPTER ONE

1. *Weekly State Journal,* (Raleigh), May 29 and June 5, 1861. An excellent treatment of this fascinating subject is David Leroy Corbitt's, *The Formation of the North Carolina Counties, 1663-1943* (Raleigh: State Department of Archives and History, 1950). It could not be determined precisely how many counties there were by reference to this study, because in listing the counties in 1850 and 1870 in chronological order, no reference is made to the years that intervened.

2. Documents in Legislative Papers, 1860-61, North Carolina Department of Archives and History at Raleigh. (Hereinafter cited as Legislative Papers).

3. Legislative Papers, 1860-61, and *Public Laws of the State of North Carolina Passed by the General Assembly at its Session of 1860-61, together with the Comptroller's Statement of Public Revenue and Expenditure* (Raleigh: John Spelman, State Printer, 1861) X, Sec. 1. (Hereinafter cited as *Laws of North Carolina*).

4. Legislative Papers, 1860-61; *Laws of North Carolina, 1860-61,* XI, Sec. 1-3.

5. Legislative Papers, 1860-61.

6. *Laws of North Carolina, 1860-61,* VIII, Sec. 1.

7. Legislative Papers, 1860-61.

8. *Laws of North Carolina, 1860-61,* VI, Sec. 1.

9. Legislative Papers, Second Extra Session, 1861.

10. *Laws of North Carolina, 1860-61,* VI, Sec. 5, 7-9.

11. *Laws of North Carolina 1860-61,* VI, Sec. 11, 14-16.

12. Legislative Papers, 1860-61, n. d.

13. *Ibid.*

14. *Western Sentinel* (Winston-Salem), April 26, 1861.

15. *Fayetteville Observer,* June 24, 1861.

16. *Fayetteville Observer,* July 8, 1861.

17. *Fayetteville Observer,* September 9, 1861.

18. *Fayetteville Observer,* July 15 and July 22, 1861.

19. Legislative Papers, 1860-61. Twenty-three counties had children in the institution, but the typewriter had not been invented and Palmer had to make the copies of his letters when it was most convenient to do so. This may account for the fact that the letters were mailed between October, 1860, and April, 1861. Manuscripts indicating that letters had been sent to the other sixteen counties could not be found.

20. Legislative Papers, 1860-61.

21. *Laws of North Carolina, 1860-61*, XXXII, Sec. 1.

22. *Public Laws of the State of North Carolina Passed by the General Assembly at its Second Extra Session of 1860-61* (Raleigh: John Spelman, State Printer, 1861), XXXI, Sec. 54, 70.

23. *Newbern Progress*, quoted in the *Weekly State Journal* (Raleigh), June 12, 1861.

24. Legislative Papers, 1860-61.

25. *Ibid.*

26. *Journal of the House of Commons of North Carolina, Session of 1860-61* (Raleigh: John Spelman, State Printer, 1861), p. 496. (Hereinafter cited as *House Journal*).

27. *Journal of the Senate of North-Carolina, at its Session of 1860-61* (Raleigh: John Spelman, State Printer, 1861), pp. 374, 375, 455. (Hereinafter cited as *Senate Journal*).

28. Legislative Papers, 1860-61. In 1789 when the United States Constitution was adopted, North Carolina was authorized to send two senators and five representatives to Congress according to constitutional apportionment. In 1792, when the first federal census had been completed and tabulated, it was found that North Carolina was entitled to ten representatives. By 1812, the North Carolina population had increased to the extent that it was entitled to thirteen representatives in Congress. Between 1812 and 1865, the population of the State decreased to such extent that in proportion to the population of the other States North Carolina was entitled to only seven representatives.

29. *Laws of North Carolina, Second Extra Session, 1861*, III, Sec. 2.

30. Legislative Papers, 1860-61.

31. *Laws of North Carolina, Second Extra Session, 1861*, XIV, Sec. 1.

32. W. T. Dortch to Speaker of the Senate, Legislative Papers, 1860-61; *House Journal, 1860-61*, p. 412; *House Journal, Second Extra Session, 1861*, pp. 56, 71, 72, 123, 124, 127, 153, 154, 160,

161, 165-67, 174, 175, 179-81, 188, 189, 192-95. For Senate election see *Senate Journal, Second Extra Session, 1861,* pp. 152, 153.

33. Legislative Papers, 1860-61; Laws of North Carolina, 1860-61, XLII; *Private Laws of North Carolina Passed by the General Assembly at its First Extra Session, 1861* (Raleigh: John Spelman, State Printer, 1861), XX. (Hereinafter cited as *Private Laws of North Carolina*).

34. *House Journal, 1860-61,* p. 198.

35. *House Journal, 1860-61,* p. 242.

36. *Senate Journal, 1860-61,* pp. 125, 126, 128.

37. *House Journal, 1860-61,* pp. 249-51, and *Senate Journal, 1860-61,* pp. 139-41.

38. *House Journal, 1860-61,* pp. 412, 414.

39. *House Journal, 1860-61,* p. 204.

40. *House Journal, 1860-61,* p. 267.

41. *Senate Journal, 1860-61,* p. 254.

42. *Weekly State Journal* (Raleigh), April 24, 1861.

43. *Ordinances and Resolutions Passed by the State Convention of North Carolina, First Session in May and June, 1861* (Raleigh: John W. Syme, Convention Printer, 1862), Ordinance 20. (Hereinafter cited as *Convention Ordinances*).

44. Legislative Papers, 1860-61.

45. *Laws of North Carolina, 1860-61,* CXLIX.

46. *Laws of North Carolina, 1860-61,* CXLVIII, Sec. 1.

47. *Laws of North Carolina 1860-61,* CL, Sec. 1, 2.

48. Eusebius Hendrick and Chapel Hendrick to the Assembly, *in* Legislative Papers, 1860-61.

49. Legislative Papers, 1860-61.

50. Henry T. Clark to Speaker of the House *in* Legislative Papers, 1860-61, and the *Church Intelligencer* (Raleigh), July 18, 1861.

51. Letters in the Governor's Papers, 1860-61, in the North Carolina Department of Archives and History at Raleigh. (Hereinafter cited as Executive Papers.)

52. Executive Papers, 1860-61.

53. Executive Papers, 1860-61.

54. Executive Papers, 1860-61.

55. Executive Papers, 1860-61.

56. Frances Timberlake to John W. Ellis in Executive Papers, 1860-61.

57. John Letcher to John W. Ellis and W. Gwynn to John W. Ellis, in Executive Papers, 1860-61.

58. M. S. Perry to John W. Ellis in Executive Papers, 1860-61.

59. V. R. Gist to John W. Ellis in Executive Papers, 1860-61.

60. T. M. Jones to John W. Ellis in Executive Papers, 1860-61.

61. H. N. Howard to J. F. Hoke in Junius Davis Papers, North Carolina Department of Archives and History at Raleigh.

62. Harry E. Cotton to John W. Ellis and Winslow, Guion, and Bradford in Executive Papers.

63. W. W. Pierce to John W. Ellis in Executive Papers.

64. N. N. Fleming to John W. Ellis in Executive Papers, 1860-61.

65. John W. Ellis to N. N. Fleming in Executive Papers, 1860-61.

66. Copy of original proclamation of Jefferson Davis, President of the Confederacy, in North Carolina Department of Archives and History, Raleigh.

67. Samuel Pearce to John W. Ellis in Executive Papers, 1860-61.

68. N. H. Whitfield to John W. Ellis in Executive Papers, 1860-61.

69. Eugene M. Williams to John W. Ellis in Executive Papers, 1860-61.

70. G. W. Blackwell to John W. Ellis in Executive Papers, 1860-61.

71. William L. Robinson to John W. Ellis in Executive Papers, 1860-61.

72. W. J. Houston to John W. Ellis in Executive Papers, 1860-61.

73. J. H. Foust to John W. Ellis in Executive Papers, 1860-61.

74. J. J. Bricknell and J P. Lovelace to John W. Ellis in Executive Papers, 1860-61.

75. J. P. Aldridge *et al.* to John W. Ellis in Executive Papers, 1860-61.

76. *Fayetteville Observer*, January 7, 1861.

77. W. R. Burbank to John W. Ellis in Executive Papers, 1860-61.

78. Executive Papers, 1860-61.

79. J. G. DeRoulhac Hamilton, *The Papers of Thomas Ruffin* (3 vols., 1859 to 1865, Raleigh: North Carolina Historical Commission) III, 175. (Hereinafter cited as *Papers of Thomas Ruffin*).

80. W. T. Dortch to Speaker of the Senate, House Resolution, undated, Second Extra Session, 1861, and Legislative Papers, 1860-61.

81. Message of Henry T. Clark to the General Assembly on August 16, 1861 (North Carolina Department of Archives and History at Raleigh). (Hereinafter cited as Henry T. Clark to General Assembly).

82. Henry T. Clark to General Assembly, September 11, 1861.

NOTES TO CHAPTER TWO

1. *Riggs* v. *Swann,* 59 North Carolina, 118.

2. Wake County Deed Book 23, p. 265. This county was typical of the five or six heavily populated, large slaveholding counties.

3. Wake County Deed Book 23, p. 313.

4. Wake County Deed Book 23, p. 275.

5. Wake County Deed Book 23, p. 271.

6. Wake County Deed Book 23, p. 375.

7. Wake County Deed Book 23, p. 505.

8. *Daily Bulletin* (Charlotte), June 19, 1861.

9. *Weekly State Journal* (Raleigh), June 5, 1861.

10. *Daily Bulletin* (Charlotte), June 19, 1861.

11. *Mountain Eagle* (Shelby), June 19, 1861.

12. *Fayetteville Observer,* October 21, 1861.

13. *Fayetteville Observer,* December 30, 1861.

14. *Fayetteville Observer,* November 18, 1861.

15. *North Carolina Presbyterian* (Fayetteville), June 30, 1860.

16. *North Carolina Presbyterian* (Fayetteville), February 2, 1861.

17. *Fayetteville Observer,* January 14, 1861.

18. *Fayetteville Observer,* March 4, 1861.

19. *Carolina Watchman* (Salisbury), May 23, 1861.

20. *Winston Sentinel* (Winston), April 19, 1861.

21. *Fayetteville Observer,* June 13, 1861.

22. *Daily Bulletin* (Charlotte), June 19, 1861.

23. *North Carolina Presbyterian* (Fayetteville), July 13, 1861.

24. *Weekly State Journal* (Raleigh), August 28 and September 4, 1861.

25. *Weekly State Journal* (Raleigh), November 28, 1860.

26. *Fayetteville Observer,* January 14, 1861.

27. *Carolina Watchman* (Salisbury) , January 15, 1861.

28. *Iredell Express,* quoted in *Greensborough Patriot,* December 6, 1860.

29. *Fayetteville Observer,* November 25, 1861.

30. *Proceedings of the Eleventh Annual Meeting of Stockholders of the Raleigh and Gaston Railroad, held at Raleigh July 4, 1861* (Raleigh: North Carolina Institute for the Deaf, Dumb, and Blind, Printer, 1861, pamphlet in N. C. Department of Archives and History, Raleigh), p. 6.

31. *Convention Ordinance 19, Second Session, 1861.*

32. J. E. B. Grimes to Major Bryan Grimes in the Bryan Grimes Collection, North Carolina Department of Archives and History at Raleigh.

33. *Papers of Thomas Ruffin,* p. 93.

34. *Papers of Thomas Ruffin,* p. 99.

35. *Papers of Thomas Ruffin,* p. 100.

36. *Papers of Thomas Ruffin,* pp. 68, 69.

37. *Private Laws of North Carolina, 1860-61,* CC, Sec. 1.

38. *Fayetteville Observer,* August 5 and 12, 1861.

39. *Fayetteville Observer,* December 23, 1861.

40. *Terest Carman* v. *Stephen Page,* 59 North Carolina, 37.

41. *David Swindall, by his next friend, William J. McNeill* v. *William Bradley,* 59 North Carolina, 41.

42. *William Norfleet and D. P. Lloyd, Executors,* v. *Helen B. Slade et al.,* 59 North Carolina, 216.

43. *Amelia Smith* v. *Leland Martin et al.,* 59 North Carolina, 179.

NOTES TO CHAPTER THREE

1. *Papers of Thomas Ruffin,* p. 81.

2. *Papers of Thomas Ruffin,* p. 83.

3. Legislative Papers, 1860-61.

4. *Papers of Thomas Ruffin,* pp. 64, 65.

5. *Winston Sentinel,* March 29, 1861.

6. *Laws of North Carolina, Second Extra Session, 1861,* XIV, Sec. 1, 2.

7. *Convention Ordinance Number 10, Second Session, 1861.*

8. *Convention Ordinance Number 13, Second Session, 1861.*

9. Legislative Papers, 1860-61; *House Journal, 1860-61,* pp. 122, 123; and *Senate Journal, 1860-61,* pp. 236, 237.

10. *Senate Journal, 1860-61,* pp. 145, 146.

11. *Senate Journal, 1860-61,* p. 150.

12. Legislative Papers, 1860-61.

13. Legislative Papers, 1860-61.

14. Secretary of State Papers, North Carolina Department of Archives and History at Raleigh.

15. Legislative Papers, 1860-61.

16. *House Journal, 1860-61,* pp. 203, 204.

17. Legislative Papers, 1860-61.

18. Legislative Papers, 1860-61.

19. Secretary of State Papers and Legislative Papers, 1860-61.

20. *Senate Journal, 1860-61,* p. 154.

21. Legislative Papers, 1860-61.

22. *House Journal, Second Extra Session, 1861,* p. 170.

23. Legislative Papers, 1860-61.

24. *Laws of North Carolina, 1860-61,* XXXVII, Sec. 1.

25. *Laws of North Carolina, 1860-61,* XXXIV, Sec. 1.

26. *Laws of North Carolina, 1860-61,* XXIII, Sec. 1, 2, 3.

27. *Laws of North Carolina, First Extra Session, 1861,* XVIII, Sec. 3.

28. *Laws of North Carolina, 1860-61,* XXXV.

29. *Laws of North Carolina, 1860-61,* XXXVI, Sec. 1, 2.

30. *Laws of North Carolina, Second Extra Session, 1861,* XVII, Sec. 9; *Convention Ordinance 8, First Session, 1861; Laws of North Carolina, Second Extra Session, 1861,* XIV, Sec. 1, 2; *Convention Ordinance 10* and *Convention Ordinance 13, Second Session, 1861.*

31. *Mountain Eagle* (Shelby), June 19, 1861.

32. *Carolina Watchman* (Salisbury), July 15, 1861.

33. George B. Johnston to Thomas Ruffin, *Papers of Thomas Ruffin,* p. 73. John W. Ellis was governor at this time, but it was the practice in North Carolina to address all former governors as governor.

34. W. R. Richardson to Thomas Ruffin, *Papers of Thomas Ruffin,* pp. 191, 192.

35. W. R. Richardson to Thomas Ruffin, *Papers of Thomas Ruffin,* p. 196.

36. Thomas Carter to Thomas Ruffin, *Papers of Thomas Ruffin*, p. 199.

37. J. W. Hall to Thomas Ruffin, *Papers of Thomas Ruffin*, p. 202.

38. Paul C. Cameron to Thomas Ruffin, *Papers of Thomas Ruffin*, p. 91.

39. Weldon N. Edwards to Thomas Ruffin, *Papers of Thomas Ruffin*, p. 101.

40. Charles Manly to Thomas Ruffin, *Papers of Thomas Ruffin*, p. 112.

41. W. C. Kerr to Thomas Ruffin, *Papers of Thomas Ruffin*, pp. 113.

42. William K. Ruffin to Thomas Ruffin, *Papers of Thomas Ruffin*, p. 127.

43. Jeremiah Holt to Thomas Ruffin, *Papers of Thomas Ruffin*, p. 175.

44. Jonathan Worth to George McNeill, Jr., *Papers of Thomas Ruffin*, pp. 74, 75.

45. George McNeill, Jr., to Thomas Ruffin, *Papers of Thomas Ruffin*, p. 73.

46. Legislative Papers, 1860-61 and *Private Laws of North Carolina, 1860-61*, CXCVIII.

47. *Winston Sentinel*, June 3, 1861.

48. *House Journal, Second Extra Session, 1861*, 170.

49. Secretary of State Papers, 1860-61.

NOTES TO CHAPTER FOUR

1. *Church Intelligencer* (Raleigh), August 30, 1860.

2. *Church Intelligencer* (Raleigh), September 20, 1860.

3. *Church Intelligencer* (Raleigh), August 2, 1861.

4. *Private Laws of North Carolina, 1860-61*, LXXII, Sec. 1-3.

5. *Private Laws of North Carolina, 1860-61*, LXXIII, Sec. 2, 5, 6; LIII, Sec. 1; and LXXIV, Sec. 2.

6. *Private Laws of North Carolina, 1860-61*, LXXIV, Sec. 2, 5, 7.

7. *Private Laws of North Carolina, 1860-61*, LII, LIV, LV, LVI, LVIII, Sec. 1, and LIX.

8. John T. Walsh (ed.), *The Carolina Christian Monthly*

(April, 1860), VIII, 49-53, in the John T. Walsh Papers, Atlantic Christian College, Wilson.

9. John T. Walsh (ed.), *The Carolina Christian Monthly*, (May, 1860), VIII, 120.

10. *Church Intelligencer* (Raleigh), August 30, 1860.

11. *Fayetteville Observer*, July 1, 1861.

12. *Weekly Message* (Greensboro), July 20, 1861.

13. *Fayetteville Observer*, September 16, 1861.

14. *Senate Journal, 1860-61*, pp. 73, 75, and *House Journal, 1860-61*, p. 89.

15. *Hillsborough Recorder*, May 1, 1861.

16. *Western Sentinel* (Winston), July 12, 1861.

17. *Fayetteville Observer*, August 12, 1861.

18. Legislative Papers, 1860-61.

19. *House Journal, 1860-61*, 685.

20. Legislative Papers, First and Second Extra Sessions, 1861.

21. *Laws of North Carolina, Second Extra Session, 1861*, IV, Sec. 1.

22. *Laws of North Carolina, Second Extra Session, 1861*, XXXI, Sec. 1.

23. *Document 10, Report of the Superintendent of Common Schools of North Carolina for the Year 1860* in *Executive and Legislative Documents, Session 1860-61, Part II* (Raleigh: John Spelman, State Printer, 1861), pp. 11-15. (Hereinafter cited as *Document 10*).

24. *Greensborough Patriot*, November 15, 1860.

25. *Western Sentinel* (Winston), November 29, 1860, and the *Greensborough Patriot*, November 22, 1860.

26. *Charlotte Democrat* in the *Carolina Watchman* (Salisbury), October 28, 1861.

27. *Document 10, Part I*, 3-6.

28. *Public Laws of North Carolina, 1860-61*, II, Sec. 1, 2, 3.

29. *Fayetteville Observer*, May 13, 1861.

30. *Fayetteville Observer*, December 2, 1861.

31. John Louis Taylor, first Chief Justice of North Carolina, opened the first law school in the State in Raleigh in 1822. The first law school affiliated with an institution was organized at the University of North Carolina in 1841, and opened in 1843 by William Horn Battle.

32. *Document 10, Part II, 7, 8; Senate Journal, 1860-61*, XXVI;

and Jacob Garrett to Thomas Ruffin, *Papers of Thomas Ruffin,* p. 199.

33. *Weekly State Journal* (Raleigh), December 5, 1860.

34. *Weekly State Journal* (Raleigh), November 28 and December 5 and 12, 1860.

35. *Executive and Legislative Documents, 1860-61,* Document 1, the Governor's Message (Raleigh: John Spelman, State Printer, 1861), pp. 7, 8, 24, 25, 30, 31.

36. *Weekly State Journal* (Raleigh), December 12, 1860.

37. *North Carolina Presbyterian* (Fayetteville), January 6, 1861.

38. *Western Sentinel* (Winston), March 15, 1861.

39. *DeBows Review,* quoted in the *Western Sentinel* (Winston), March 22, 1861.

40. *Mountain Eagle* (Shelby), January 19, 1861, and the *Belton* (Texas) *Independent,* June 4, 1861, quoted in *Mountain Eagle* (Shelby), June 19, 1861.

41. *Church Intelligencer* (Raleigh), October 4, 1861.

NOTES TO CHAPTER FIVE

1. See especially *Carolina Watchman* (Salisbury), quoted in the *North Carolina Presbyterian* (Fayetteville), July 13, 1861.

2. Unpublished Census Report for 1860. (Mf. 57, Religious Census in North Carolina, Department of Archives and History, Raleigh). Hereinafter cited as Religious Census. The Unpublished Census is the best and most complete source of religious statistics, but obviously this schedule should have been more carefully constructed and steps taken to assure more uniform reporting.

3. *Goldsboro Tribune* in *The United States Catholic Miscellany* (Charleston, S. C.), September 7, 1861.

4. *The United States Catholic Miscellany* (Charleston, S. C.), September 7, 1861.

5. *Goldsboro Tribune* in *The United States Catholic Miscellany* (Charleston, S. C.), September 28, 1861.

6. *Church Intelligencer* (Raleigh), August 2, 1861.

7. *Minutes of the General Assembly of the Presbyterian Church in the Confederate States of America,* (Augusta, Georgia: Steam Power Press Chronicle and Sentinel, 1861) , I 43. (Hereinafter cited as *Presbyterian Minutes*).

8. The Papers of Hariot Clarkson in the North Carolina Department of Archives and History at Raleigh.

9. *Presbyterian Minutes,* p. 43.

10. *Presbyterian Minutes,* p. 58.

11. Original Minute Book of the Meherrin Baptist Church in North Carolina Department of Archives and History at Raleigh, p. 208. (Hereinafter cited as *Meherrin Minutes*).

12. *Meherrin Minutes, 1861.*

13. Records of the Lufty Baptist Church, Great Smokey Mountains National Park. (Mf. 58 in North Carolina Department of Archives and History at Raleigh).

14. Minutes of the Wheeler's Primitive Baptist Church at Yanceville, 1790-1898, copied by John Birch Blalock in North Carolina Department of Archives and History at Raleigh.

15. *Minutes of the One Hundred Third Session of the Stony Creek Baptist Association held with the Church at Mt. Vernon Springs, Chatham County, North Carolina, October 4-7, 1861* (Raleigh: *Biblical Recorder,* Association Printer, 1861) p. 6. (Hereinafter cited as *Sandy Creek Minutes*) .

16. *Minutes of the Seventh Annual Session of the Brown Creek Baptist Association, held with the Church at Philadelphia, Union County, North Carolina, October 11, 12, and 14, 1861* (Raleigh: *Biblical Recorder,* Association Printer, 1861), p. 14. (Hereinafter cited as *Brown Creek Minutes*).

17. *Minutes of the Sixty Eighth Annual Session of the Yadkin Baptist Association, held with the Eaton's Church, Davie County, North Carolina, October Fifth to Eighth, 1860* (Salem: L. V. and E. T. Blum, Association Printers, 1860), p. 7.

18. *Yadkin Minutes,* p. 8.

19. *Meherrin Minutes, 1860.* See especially pp. 207, 208.

20. *Meherrin Minutes, 1861.*

21. Minutes of the Three Forks Baptist Church, Boone, 1790-1895 (Mf. 60 in the North Carolina Department of Archives and History at Raleigh. Hereinafter cited as *Three Forks Minutes*).

22. *The Primitive Baptist* (Melbornie) July 27, 1861 (Mf. 87

in North Carolina Department of Archives and History at Raleigh).

23. *Minutes of the Fifty Fourth Annual Session of the Chowan Baptist Association, held with the Church in Edenton, North Carolina, May 15-19, 1860* (Murfreesboro: S. J. Wheeler, Clerk, 1860), p. 21. (Hereinafter cited as *Chowan Minutes*).

24. *Yadkin Minutes, 1860,* p. 13.

25. *Minutes of the Twenty Nineth Session of the Liberty Baptist Association, held at Lick Creek Meeting House, Davidson County, North Carolina, August 23d, 24th and 26th, 1861* (Salisbury: J. J. Stewart, Association Printer, 1861), pp. 8, 9. (Hereinafter cited as *Liberty Minutes*).

26. *Brown Creek Minutes, 1861,* pp. 6, 7.

27. *Chowan Minutes, 1860,* pp. 16, 19.

28. *Meherrin Minutes, 1860,* pp. 205, 206.

29. *Minutes of the Twenty Seventh Annual Session of the Beulah Baptist Association, held with the Church at Hillsborough, North Carolina, August 10-13, 1860* (Raleigh: *Biblical Recorder,* Association Printer, 1860), p. 6. (Hereinafter cited as *Beulah Minutes*).

30. *Minutes of the Seventeenth Annual Session of the Union Baptist Association, held with the Church at Lebanon, New Hanover County, North Carolina, October 9-12, 1860* (Raleigh: *Biblical Recorder,* Association Printer, 1860), p. 36. (Hereinafter cited as *Union Minutes*).

31. *Minutes of the Thirteenth Annual Session of the Tar River Baptist Association, held with the Church at Franklinton, Franklin County, North Carolina, August 23, 24, 25, 1860* (Raleigh: *Biblical Recorder,* Association Printer, 1860), p. 5. (Hereinafter cited as *Tar River Minutes*).

32. *Proceedings of the Sandy Creek Baptist Association, held with the Church at Gum Springs, Chatham County, North Carolina, October 2, 1860* (n.d., n.p.,), pp. 10, 11. (Hereinafter cited as *Sandy Creek Minutes*).

33. *Minutes of the Tenth Annual Session of the Pamlico Baptist Association, held with the Church at Conconary, Halifax County, North Carolina, October 18-20, 1860* (Raleigh: *Biblical Recorder,* Association Printer, 1860), p. 13. (Hereinafter cited as *Pamlico Minutes*).

34. *Minutes of the Third Session of the Cedar Creek Baptist*

Association, held at Baptist Chapel Church, Sampson County, North Carolina, November 8th, 9th, 10th, 11th, 1860 (Fayetteville: Edward J. Hale and Sons, Association Printers, 1860), p. 8. (Hereinafter cited as *Cedar Creek Minutes*).

35. *Brown Creek Minutes, 1861*, pp. 7, 8.

36. *Minutes of the Fifty Seventh Session of the Cape Fear Baptist Association, held with the Church at Antioch, Robeson County, North Carolina, October 25, 26, 27, and 28, 1861* (Fayetteville: Edward J. Hale, Association Printer, 1862), pp. 8, 9. (Hereinafter cited as *Cape Fear Minutes*).

37. *Liberty Minutes, 1861,* pp. 6, 7.

38. *Minutes of the French Broad Baptist Church, Mill River,* (Mf. 49 in the North Carolina Department of Archives and History at Raleigh).

39. *Minutes of the Second Annual Session of the United Baptist Association, held with Concord Church, Alexander County, North Carolina, October 18th, 19th, and 20th, 1861* (Salem: L. V. and E. T. Blum, Association Printers, 1861), p. 12.

40. *Pamlico Minutes, 1860,* p. 6.

41. *Minutes and Proceedings of the Forty Fifth Anniversary of the Pee Dee Baptist Association, held with the Church at Forks of Little River, Montgomery County, North Carolina, October 20-22, 1860* (Fayetteville: Edward J. Hale and Sons, 1860), p. 16.

42. *Liberty Minutes, 1860,* p. 16.

43. *Union Minutes, 1860,* pp. 12, 16.

44. *Minutes of the Eighth Annual Session of the Pamlico Baptist Association, held with the Church at Bear Creek, Lenoir County, North Carolina, September 13, 14, 1861* (Raleigh: *Biblical Recorder,* Association Printer, 1861), p. 12.

45. *Minutes of the Thirty First Annual Session of the Tar River Baptist Association, held with the Church at Maple Springs in Franklin County, North Carolina, August 22, 23, 24, 1861* (Raleigh: *Biblical Recorder,* Association Printer, 1861), p. 21.

46. *The Carolina Christian Monthly*, VIII, No. 1 (January 1860), 19, 20.

47. *Journal of the General Conference of the Methodist Episcopal Church, held in Buffaloe, New York, 1860* (New York: Carlton and Porter, 1860).

48. George Peck, ed., *Methodist Almanac for the year of our Lord 1860* (New York: Carlton and Porter, 1861), pp. 19, 26.

(Hereinafter cited as *Methodist Almanac*), and *Minutes of the Annual Conference of the Methodist Episcopal Church, South, for the Year 1860* (Nashville, Tennessee: Southern Methodist Publishing House, 1870), p. 249. (Hereinafter cited as *Minutes of the M. E. Church, South*).

49. *Minutes of the M. E. Church, South, 1860*. See especially p. 293. It is not certain whether Portsmouth was in the North Carolina Conference in 1860, but it was reported in that Conference in 1861.

50. *Minutes of the M. E. Church, South, 1860*, p. 248.

51. *Minutes of the M. E. Church, South, 1860*, pp. 248-50.

52. *Minutes of the M. E. Church, South, 1861*, p 332.

53. *Methodist Almanac, 1861*, p. 26.

54. *Minutes of the M. E. Church, South, 1861*, pp. 310, 311.

55. *Minutes of the M. E. Church, South, 1861*, p. 332.

56. *Minutes of the Twenty Fourth Session of the North Carolina Conference of the Methodist Episcopal Church, South, held at Salisbury, North Carolina, December 5-11, 1860* (Raleigh: Strother and Marcom, 1861), pp. 13, 16.

57. *Minutes of the Thirty Fifth Session of the North Carolina Annual Conference of the Methodist Protestant Church held at Yadkin Institute, Davidson County, November 14-20, 1860* (Raleigh: Strother and Marcom Book and Job Printers, 1861), pp. 3, 4, 10, 28. (Hereinafter cited as *Methodist Protestant Minutes*).

58. *Methodist Protestant Minutes, 1860*, pp. 14, 15, 20.

59. *Minutes of the North Carolina Yearly Meeting of Friends, held at New Garden, from the 5th to 9th of Eleventh Month Inclusive, 1860* (Greensboro: Sherwood and Long, Convention Printers, 1860), p. 7. (Hereinafter cited as *Friends Minutes, 1860*).

60. *Minutes of the North Carolina Yearly Meeting of Friends, held at New Garden on the Second Day to the 4th of Eleventh Month, Inclusive, 1861* (Greensboro: Sherwood and Long, Convention Printers, 1861), p. 3. (Hereinafter cited as *Friends Minutes, 1861*).

61. *Friends Minutes, 1860*, pp. 9, 10.

62. *Friends Minutes, 1860*, pp. 4, 5.

63. *Friends Minutes, 1860*, pp. 4, 10-12, 14; *Friends Minutes, 1861*, p. 1.

64. *A Narrative of Cruelties Inflicted Upon Friends of North Carolina 1861 to 1865, in Consequence of their Faithfulness to*

the Christian View of the Unlawfulness of War, (Published by order of the Representatives of North Carolina Yearly Meeting of Friends, with an introduction by Joseph Crossfield who prepared it. London: Edward Newman, Convention Printer, 1868), pp. 8, 9.

65. *Dunigan's American Catholic Almanac, 1860,* (New York: E. Dunigan and Brother, n. d.), p. 119. (Hereinafter cited as *Catholic Almanac*).

66. Religious Census, 1860.

67. *Catholic Almanac, 1860,* p. 120.

68. *Metropolitan Catholic Almanac and Laity Directory of the United States, Canada, and the British Provinces, 1861* (Baltimore: John Murphy and Company, 1860), pp. 79, 80.

69. *The United States Catholic Miscellany* (Charleston, S. C.), April 7 and June 16, 1860, and the *Biblical Recorder* (Raleigh), June 7, 1860.

70. Executive Papers, 1860-61.

71. Hough Downing to John W. Ellis in Executive Papers, 1860-61.

72. *Fayetteville Observer,* May 20, 1861.

NOTES TO CHAPTER SIX

1. *Document 3, Second Extra Session, 1861, Table of Population of North Carolina According to the Eighth Census, Arranged by Counties Alphabetically* (n. p.: John Spelman, State Printer, n. d.); James McNeill to *North Carolina Presbyterian* in Worth Collection, North Carolina Department of Archives and History, Raleigh; *Fayetteville Observer,* December 9, 1861; Jonathan Worth to J. J. Jackson in Worth Collection; and Legislative Papers, 1860-61.

2. John C. Rives, editor and publisher, *The Congressional Globe, Containing the Debates and Proceedings of the First Session of the Thirty Sixth Congress, also the Special Session of the Senate* (Washington: John C. Rives, 1860), p. 1447. (Hereinafter cited as *Congressional Globe*).

3. *Congressional Globe, 1860-61,* pp. 1448, 1449.

4. *Congressional Globe, 1860-61,* p. 1453.

5. *Congressional Globe, 1860-61,* p. 1451.

6. H. C. Douglas to W. A. Graham in Personal Collections, North Carolina Department of Archives and History, Raleigh;

7. *House Journal, 1860-61,* pp. 47, 49, 50.

8. Jonathan Worth to J. J. Jackson in Personal Collections, North Carolina Department of Archives and History, Raleigh, and Legislative Papers, 1860-61.

9. Legislative Papers, 1860-61. This report was not to be sent to the other Raleigh newspapers, because in 1861 twenty-eight of the forty-one newspapers classified according to policy were pro-Confederate and thirteen pro-Union. Nineteen of the pro-Confederate newspapers were Democratic, six Whig, and three were "neutral' or independent. Eleven of the pro-Union newspapers were Whig papers and two were Democratic. (*Winston Sentinel,* April 19, 1861).

10. *Document 10, 1860-61,* p. 9.

11. Kenneth Rayner to Thomas Ruffin, *Papers of Thomas Ruffin,* p. 109.

12. *Fayetteville Observer,* January 14, 1861, and *Senate Journal, 1860-61,* pp. 160, 161.

13. *Fayetteville Observer,* January 21, 1861.

14. *Semi-Weekly Raleigh Register,* February 9, 1861, *Acts and Resolutions of the First Session of the Provisional Congress of the Confederate States, Held at Montgomery, Alabama,* (Richmond: Enquirer Book and Job Press, by Tyler, Wise, Allegre, and Smith, 1861), p. 6; *Public Resolutions of North Carolina, 1860-61,* January 29, 1861.

15. *Congressional Globe, 1860-61,* p. 1045.

16. *Congressional Globe, 1860-61,* pp. 1453, 1454.

17. *Semi-Weekly Raleigh Register,* February 23, 1861.

18. *Carolina Watchman* (Salisbury), February 26, 1861.

19. *Fayetteville Observer* quoted in the *Carolina Watchman* (Salisbury), March 5, 1861.

20. Legislative Papers, 1860-61.

21. Legislative Papers, 1860-61.

22. *Semi-Weekly Raleigh Register,* January 5, 1861.

23. *Semi-Weekly Raleigh Register,* January 9, 1861.

24. Legislative Papers, 1860-61.

25. Legislative Papers, 1860-61.

26. *Fayetteville Observer,* January 7, 1861.

27. *State Journal* (Raleigh), quoted in the *Western Sentinel* (Winston), April 5, 1861.

28. *Semi-Weekly Raleigh Register*, January 12, 1861.

29. Paul C. Cameron to Thomas Ruffin in *Papers of Thomas Ruffin*, p. 99.

30. *Senate Journal, 1860-61*, 100, and original resolution in Legislative Papers, 1860-61.

31. *Senate Journal, 1860-61*, p. 162.

32. *Senate Journal, 1860-61*, p. 163.

33. Legislative Papers, 1860-61; *Public Resolutions of North Carolina*, January 29, 1861; *Public Resolutions of North Carolina*, May 8, 1861; and the *Milton Chronicle*, June 28, 1861.

34. *Congressional Globe, 1860-61*, p. 497.

35. *Congressional Globe, 1860-61*, p. 476.

36. *Congressional Globe, 1860-61*, pp. 366, 605, 606.

37. *Congressional Globe, 1860-61*, p. 624.

38. *Congressional Globe, Appendix, 1860-61*, pp. 196-99.

39. *Congressional Globe, Appendix, 1860-61*, pp. 205-7.

40. Rufus S. Tucker to Thomas Ruffin in *Papers of Thomas Ruffin*, p. 114, and Cadwallader Jones, Jr., to Thomas Ruffin, *Papers of Thomas Ruffin*, p. 115. David S. Reid instead of Edgar G. Reid was selected.

41. Paul C. Cameron to Thomas Ruffin in *Papers of Thomas Ruffin*, p. 116.

42. Legislative Papers, 1860-61.

43. Executive Papers, 1860-61.

44. John Tyler to Thomas Ruffin in *Papers of Thomas Ruffin*, p. 120.

45. John M. Moreland to Thomas Ruffin in *Papers of Thomas Ruffin*, p. 139.

46. Edward Sturdwick to Thomas Ruffin in *Papers of Thomas Ruffin*, p. 117.

47. *Congressional Globe, 1860-61*, pp. 732-37.

48. *Congressional Globe, 1860-61*, pp. 196, 197.

49. *Congressional Globe, 1860-61*, p. 836.

50. *Congressional Globe, 1860-61*, pp. 853-54.

NOTES TO CHAPTER SEVEN

1. Legislative Papers, 1860-61.

2. Metthias E. Manly to Thomas Ruffin, *Papers of Thomas Ruffin,* p. 104.

3. *Senate Journal, 1860-61,* p. 143; *Semi-Weekly Raleigh Register,* January 26, 1861.

4. *Weekly State Journal* (Raleigh), December 5, 1860.

5. Legislative Papers, 1860-61.

6. *Weekly State Journal* (Raleigh), December 5, 1860.

7. Legislative Papers, 1860-61.

8. *Fayetteville Observer,* December 24, 1860.

9. William A. Graham Papers, North Carolina Department of Archives and History, Raleigh.

10. Legislative Papers, 1860-61.

11. *Congressional Globe, 1860-61,* pp. 624-26.

12. *Congressional Globe, 1860-61,* pp. 226, 228.

13. *Weekly State Journal* (Raleigh), April 3, 1861.

14. *Winston Sentinel,* March 22, 1861.

15. *Tarboro Mercury,* April 3, 1861.

16. *Weekly State Journal* (Raleigh), April 3, 1861.

17. *Winston Sentinel,* April 26, 1861.

18. *Semi-Weekly Raleigh Register,* April 17, 1861; *Weekly State Journal* (Raleigh), April 17, 1861; *House Journal, 1860-61,* pp. 124, 269, 270; *Senate Journal, 1860-61,* p. 105; *Laws of North Carolina, First Extra Session, 1861,* XVII, Sec. 1, 2, 7, 8; *Public Resolutions of North Carolina, First Extra Session, 1861,* February 2, 1861; and Legislative Papers, 1860-61.

19. *House Journal* and *Senate Journal, First Extra Session, 1861,* pp. 3, 4.

20. *Laws of North Carolina, First Extra Session, 1861,* IX, Sec. 1, 4. See also Legislative Papers, 1860-61.

21. Legislative Papers, 1860-61. A list of delegates to the State convention and a copy of the ordinance dissolving the Union between North Carolina and the United States and ratifying the Constitution of the Confederate States are found in the *Fayetteville Observer,* May 27, 1861. A list of the Assembly delegates for 1860-61 and the Convention delegates are found in the *Fayetteville Observer,* December 30, 1861.

22. *Semi-Weekly Raleigh Register,* May 15, 1861.

23. T. L. Clingman to John W. Ellis, telegram in Confederate Museum at Richmond, Virginia.

24. *Journal of the Convention of the People of North Carolina, held on the 20th Day of May, A. D., 1861* (Raleigh: John W. Syme, Convention Printer, 1862), pp. 3-5, 9.

25. *Hillsboro Recorder,* May 1, 1861.

26. John C. McRae to John W. Ellis, telegram in Confederate Museum, Richmond, Virginia.

27. Jefferson Davis to John W. Ellis, telegram in Confederate Museum, Richmond, Virginia.

28. John C. McRae to John W. Ellis, telegram in Confederate Museum, Richmond, Virginia.

29. John H. Wheeler to Thomas Ruffin in *Papers of Thomas Ruffin,* p. 151, and Bartholomew Fuller to Thomas Ruffin in *Papers of Thomas Ruffin,* p. 151.

30. *Public Resolutions of North Carolina, First Extra Session, 1861,* May 9, 1861, and Legislative Papers, 1861.

31. *Public Resolutions of North Carolina, First Extra Session, 1861,* May 11, 1861.

32. *Winston Sentinel,* April 5, 1861.

33. Legislative Papers, 1860-61.

34. *Ordinances and Resolutions Passed by the State Convention of North Carolina, First Session in May and June, 1861* (Raleigh: John W. Syme, Convention Printer, 1862), Number 16. (Hereinafter cited as *Convention Ordinances*).

35. *Convention Ordinances, First Session,* Number 14.

36. *Convention Ordinances, First Session,* Number 27.

37. *Convention Ordinances, First Session,* Number 29.

38. *North Carolina Presbyterian* (Fayetteville), July 13, 1861.

39. Legislative Papers, 1860-61.

40. Legislative Papers, 1860-61.

41. *Laws of North Carolina, Second Extra Session, 1861,* XXIII.

42. *Laws of North Carolina, Second Extra Session, 1861,* XXV.

43. *Church Intelligencer* (Raleigh), June 13, 1861.

44. *Fayetteville Observer,* July 11, 1861.

45. Legislative Papers, 1860-61, and *House Journal, First Extra Session, 1861,* pp. 57, 58, 65.

46. Legislative Papers, 1860-61.

47. *Convention Ordinances, First Session, 1861,* Number 2.

48. Jefferson Davis to W. N. Edwards in Legislative Papers, 1860-61.

49. *Convention Ordinances, First Session, 1861,* Number 29.

50. *Senate Journal, 1860-61,* pp. 110, 111.

51. *Senate Journal, 1860-61,* pp. 153, 154.

52. Legislative Papers, 1860-61. Mississippi seceded on January 9 and Florida on January 10. Information that Mississippi had seceded perhaps reached Raleigh after North Carolina had been informed of Florida's secession.

53. *Senate Journal, First Extra Session, 1861,* pp. 6, 7.

54. *Public Resolutions of North Carolina, First Extra Session, 1861,* May 9, 1861, and Legislative Papers, 1860-61.

55. W. Whitaker, Jr. to N. M. Fleming, and John W. Ellis to W. Whitaker, Jr., in Executive Papers, 1860-61, and Legislative Papers, 1860-61. Whitaker's letter was signed W. Whitaker, while the resolution favored W. W. Whitaker

56. William B. Gulich to John W. Ellis in Executive Papers, 1860-61.

57. Legislative Papers, 1860-61.

58. James Ross Snowden to G. W. Caldwell in Executive Papers.

59. John Phelan to John W. Ellis in Executive Papers.

60. J. H. Gibbon to John W. Ellis in Executive Papers.

61. G. W. Caldwell to John W. Ellis in Executive Papers.

62. Report of the Mint at Charlotte for the Quarter Ending June 30, 1861, by G. W. Caldwell, in Executive Papers.

63. Executive Papers, 1860-61.

64. H. P. White to John W. Ellis in Executive Papers, 1860-61.

65. A. Dixon to John W. Ellis in Executive Papers, 1860-61.

66. Legislative Papers, 1860-61.

67. *Public Resolutions of North Carolina, First Extra Session, 1861,* May 11, 1861.

NOTES TO CHAPTER EIGHT

1. *Asheville News,* January 5, 1860.

2. *Asheville News,* January 12, 1860.

3. *Asheville News,* January 19, 1860, and the *Salisbury Banner,* quoted in the *Asheville News,* January 19, 1960.

4. *Asheville News,* January 26, 1860.

5. *Asheville News,* November 1, 1860.

6. *Senate Journal, 1860-61,* pp. 146, 147; Legislative Papers, 1860-61.

7. *Senate Journal, 1860-61,* p. 158.

8. *Senate Journal, 1860-61,* pp. 158-61; Legislative Papers, 1860-61.

9. John W. Ellis to John L. Cantwell, *Document 28, The North Carolina Forts, Report of John W. Ellis, in Executive and Legislative Documents, 1860-61* (Raleigh: John Spelman, State Printer, 1861), p. 6. (Hereinafter cited as *Document 28*).

10. John L. Cantwell to John W. Ellis, *Document 28*, p. 7.

11. J. L. Cantwell to J. J. Hendrick, *Document 28*, p. 8.

12. John J. Hendrick to John L. Cantwell, *Document 28*, p. 8, and Legislative Papers, 1860-61.

13. John W. Ellis to James Buchanan, *Document 28*, p. 1.

14. J. Holt to John W. Ellis, *Document 28*, p. 5.

15. J. Holt to John W. Ellis, Executive Papers, 1860-61.

16. Legislative Papers, 1860-61.

17. *Senate Journal, 1860-61,* p. 161.

18. S. I. Person to John W. Ellis, telegram in Confederate Museum, Richmond, Virginia.

19. F. L. Clingman to John W. Ellis, telegram in Confederate Museum, Richmond, Virginia.

20. Telegram to John W. Ellis in Confederate Museum at Richmond. The signature is not legible.

21. *Western Sentinel* (Winston), May 3, 1861.

22. Legislative Papers, 1860-61.

23. *Public Resolutions of North Carolina, First Extra Session, 1861,* May 9, 1861.

24. *Laws of North Carolina, 1860-61,* XXVII, Sec. 1, 3, and D. H. Hill to John W. Ellis, F. W. Pickins to John W. Ellis, and Horace Mayfield to John W. Ellis, telegrams in Confederate Museum at Richmond, Virginia.

25. *Public Resolutions of North Carolina, First Extra Session, 1861,* May 4, 1861.

26. *Laws of North Carolina, First Extra Session, 1861,* III, Sec. 1, 2.

27. *Public Resolutions of North Carolina, First Extra Session, 1861,* May 10, 1861.

28. *Public Resolutions of North Carolina, First Extra Session, 1861*, May 11, 1861.

29. *Public Resolutions of North Carolina, Second Extra Session, 1861*, August 30, 1861, and *Laws of North Carolina, Second Extra Session, 1861*, XVIII, Sec. 1.

30. *Laws of North Carolina, Second Extra Session, 1861*, XXXI.

31. *Convention Ordinances, Number 16, Second Session, 1861*.

32. *Weekly State Journal* (Raleigh), June 12 and 19, 1861.

33. *Private Laws of North Carolina, Second Extra Session, 1861*, XXXVIII.

34. *Private Laws of North Carolina, Second Extra Session, 1861*, XLV, Sec. 1, 2.

35. *Private Laws of North Carolina, Second Extra Session, 1861*, LX, Sec. 1-3.

36. *Private Laws of North Carolina, Second Extra Session, 1861*, LXX, Sec. 1-3.

37. *Public Resolutions of North Carolina, Second Extra Session, 1861*, September 20, 1861.

38. Edward Cantwell to William J. Dortch and William J. Dortch to Henry T. Clark in Legislative Papers, 1860-61; Legislative Papers, 1860-61 and 1861-62; and Jonathan Worth to H. B. Elliott, Jonathan Worth to B. G. Worth, and Jonathan Worth to H. B. Elliott in Jonathan Worth Collection, North Carolina Department of Archives and History, Raleigh. In comparison with the average price of slaves in 1861, even to the casual observer, $2,500 seems to be excessive. However, it was the State, not the slaveholder, who was then facing soil exhaustion, falling cotton prices, and consequent bankruptcy, which was compensating for this loss. Perhaps this price was the State's answer to the growing disregard for slave property in the North.

39. *Public Resolutions of North Carolina, Second Extra Session, 1861*, September 21, 1861.

40. *Western Sentinel*, (Winston), May 10, 1861.

41. *Raleigh Register*, quoted in the *Western Sentinel*, May 3, 1861.

42. *Public Resolutions of North Carolina, First Extra Session, 1861*, May 11, 1861.

43. Kenneth Rayner to Thomas Ruffin in *Papers of Thomas Ruffin*, p. 173.

44. *Weekly State Journal* (Raleigh), July 31, 1861.

45. W. T. Dortch to Henry T. Clark, Legislative Papers, 1860-61.

46. Henry T. Clark to Speaker of the House, Legislative Papers, 1860-61.

47. L. O. B. Branch to Henry T. Clark, and A. C. Myers to L. O. B. Branch, Legislative Papers, 1860-61.

48. *Public Resolutions of North Carolina, Second Extra Session, 1861*, September 13, 1861.

49. Henry T. Clark to General Assembly, Legislative Papers, 1860-61.

50. *Laws of North Carolina, First Extra Session, 1861*, IV, Sec. 1-8.

51. *Laws of North Carolina, First Extra Session, 1861*, XXXIV, Sec. 1-3.

52. *Laws of North Carolina, Second Extra Session, 1861*, XV, Sec. 1.

53. *Laws of North Carolina, Second Extra Session, 1861*, XVIII, Sec. 1.

54. *Private Laws of North Carolina, Second Extra Session, 1861*, XXXII.

55. *Public Resolutions of North Carolina, Second Extra Session, 1861*, September 13, 1861.

56. Legislative Papers, 1860-61.

57. *Fayetteville Observer*, August 5 and September 19, 1861.

58. Legislative Papers, 1860-61.

59. *Weekly State Journal* quoted in the *Western Sentinel* (Winston), May 10, 1861.

60. *Fayetteville Observer*, July 29, 1861.

61. *Weekly State Journal* (Raleigh), October 9, 1861.

62. Legislative Papers, 1861-62.

63. *Convention Ordinance 27, First Session, 1861*.

64. *Carolina Watchman* (Salisbury), August 1, 1861.

65. *Weekly State Journal* (Raleigh), September 4, 1861.

66. *Carolina Watchman* (Salisbury), November 4, 1861.

67. *Carolina Watchman* (Salisbury), June 6, 1861.

68. Kenneth Rayner to Justices of the Peace of Hertford County, the Kenneth Rayner Papers, in the North Carolina Department of Archives and History, Raleigh.

69. Legislative Papers, 1860-61.

70. *Fayetteville Observer,* November 25, 1861.

71. *Daily Bulletin* (Charlotte), June 19, 1861.

72. *Fayetteville Observer,* June 10, 1861.

73. *Fayetteville Observer,* June 13, 1861.

74. *Fayetteville Observer,* January 21, 1861.

75. *House Journal,* 1860-61, pp. 197, 198.

76. *Document 29, Report of John W. Ellis on the cost of an Armory, in Executive and Legislative Documents, Session of 1860-61* (Raleigh: John Spelman, State Printer), pp. 1-4.

77. *Western Sentinel* (Winston), April 26, 1861.

78. Legislative Papers, 1860-61.

79. *Laws of North Carolina, Second Extra Session, 1861,* II, Sec. 1.

80. *Private Laws of North Carolina, Second Extra Session, 1861,* XXXVI, Sec. 5.

81. *Nashville Union* quoted in the *Fayetteville Observer,* July 1, 1861.

82. *Wilmington Journal* quoted in the *Fayetteville Observer,* June 10, 1861.

83. *Convention Ordinance 8, Second Session, 1861,* Sec. 1, 2, 6, 10.

Index